I0039546

What People Are Saying About *Soul Rape*

"After the jolting ride of reading Dr. Heyward B. Ewart's book, one thing that comes to mind is that hope remains despite the most despicable forms of abuse. This hope lies in the recognition of a loving God who continues to cause even the most wounded hearts to continue beating. To me, as a physician, the miraculous and beautiful human heart is evidence of God's own existence. A throbbing heart is a ready reminder of God. *Soul Rape* is an eye-opener for everybody who hates human suffering. It clearly demonstrates that mental illness is usually the result of being sinned against. We need to stop this cycle of abuse, which is occurring not just often but virtually all the time all around this world. The first step is to master the insights of this invaluable book, which is destined to change the face of psychology and theology permanently."

Anacleto B. Millendez, M.D., Founder, Beautiful Heart Foundation
Medical Director, Center for Holistic, Alternative & Restorative
Medicine (CHARM)

"*Soul Rape* is a *tour de force* of the tortured landscape of child abuse and its pernicious long-term outcomes. Numerous case studies expertly intertwine with theoretical insights to produce the equivalent of a comprehensive and unconventional treatment modality. This book is an important contribution toward the edification of victims and institutions alike."

—Sam Vaknin, PhD, author *Malignant Self-Love*

"You bring out some very enlightening experiences that certainly back up your theories. Having worked in both a county mental-health clinic and an 800-bed mental health facility, I found your compassion and unique style of therapy refreshing."

—Pam English, mental health professional

"I will recommend your book to everyone on our mailing list. I would agree that child abuse has a major influence on the development of one's personality... living in an abusive environment tends to [make a child] unable to explore or discover his or her own self."

—Cynthia F. Parry, PhD

"This is a wonderful book. It should be compulsory reading for anyone dealing with abused children or abused adults, or adult survivors of childhood abuse: physicians, psychologists, and other therapists, teachers, protective workers, and so on. And the language is so clear and non-technical that it will be of enormous benefit to the survivors of trauma themselves, and even to parents who want to ensure the safety and wellbeing of their children."

—Robert Rich, PhD

"Heyward Bruce Ewart created [this book] to help victims, parents and therapists. There are various tests included in this book which can help determine whether the victim is suffering from Post Traumatic Stress Disorder. There is a test for concealed child abuse and a domestic violence inventory questionnaire throughout its pages, descriptions of what effects the abuse has taken and how you can break free. This book is not meant to take over the work of a qualified therapist, but to help therapists and those dealing with abused people. This book is an excellent resource!"

—Lori Plach for *Reader Views*

"The book provides the reader with an in depth understanding into the long-lasting effects of abuse and also provides a number useful tests and tools to aid in such areas as uncovering concealed child abuse and screening for potentially dangerous employees. This is an important book and would be a beneficial read for those who were abused as children, those currently suffering from abuse, those working with the abused, and anyone who knows someone who has been abused."

—Kam Aures for *Rebeccas Reads*

"I have found that almost two thirds of the women that I have interviewed present a long history of abuse as the main etiology of their depression. I will translate your tests and use them in my practice."

—Ricardo Villamizar, Clinical Psychologist,
Marin General Hospital, Ecuador

"I am currently working on a USAID-funded Women's Health and Family Welfare Project in Indonesia. We are very interested in using your tests on child abuse and domestic violence and will translate them."

—Harriet Beazley, PhD,
Women's Health & Family Welfare Project, Indonesia

"I used to be a social worker. It is an unfortunate fact of life that abuse is prevalent today, and has been for some time. I do know that things have changed slightly for the better, as understanding of the effects of abuse have significantly improved. That said, much remains to be done.

Perhaps one of the toughest parts of dealing with clients, abused, abuser, and family members of both; is getting them to understand the far reaching consequences of abuse. The author, Heyward Ewart III, does an excellent job of illustrating just what some of these consequences are for all involved. Through the use of case studies, discussion and review of psychological theory, and information of on-going research; the author offers hope of healing and working through the abuse for all involved.

There are numerous tests, checklists and questionnaires included. These are extremely useful to the layperson, qualified counselor, student and family members. Anyone in the field of psychotherapy or counseling will find this book extremely helpful. Some of the areas, of course, are simply review of theory and information already known widely. But even for the long-term counselor there is new information to be gleaned. I consider this work to be an important new addition to the field of study of abuse. If you have a family member who has suffered abuse, or been abused yourself, you will find much here to help you.

I admire the author's ability to speak to all levels of interested people who will be reading this book. I think no one will be confused, or feel that he is talking 'down' to you, or dumbing down the info to make it easier to understand. His forthright manner and detailed writing style will make this book informative and useful to anyone in the field or with an interest in the long term effects of abuse.

It is definitely a book that will be referred to again and again by all users. I look forward to reading additional material by this author."

Lauri C. Coates for *ReviewTheBook.com*

"It is, indeed, kind of you to make available your inventories for measuring domestic violence against both women and children. I am a Health Social Scientist from India and will conduct some reliability studies here."

—Hemant Kulkarni, MD

"I have frequent contact with both elementary school age children and with unwed mothers, many of whom I suspect were sexually abused as children. I am sure your work will be helpful."

—Barbara Franks-Morra, RN, MFA

SOUL RAPE
Recovering Personhood after Abuse

Heyward Bruce Ewart, Ph.D., D.D.

Foreword by W.E. Krill, Jr., M.S.P.C.

New Horizons in Therapy Series

Originally published as
AM I BAD? Recovering From Abuse

Soul Rape: Recovering Personhood After Abuse
Copyright © 2012 Heyward Bruce Ewart, Ph.D., D.D.

From the New Horizons in Therapy Series

No part of this publication may be reproduced, transmitted in any form or by
any means, electronic, mechanical, photocopying, recording, or otherwise, or
stored in a retrieval system, without the prior written consent of the publisher.

Library of Congress Cataloging-in-Publication Data

Ewart, Heyward Bruce, 1943-
  Soul rape : recovering personhood after abuse / Heyward Bruce Ewart ;
foreword by W.E. Krill, Jr.
      p. cm. -- (New horizons in therapy series)
  Includes bibliographical references and index.
  ISBN 978-1-61599-167-9 (hardcover : alk. paper) -- ISBN 978-1-61599-168-6
(pbk. : alk. paper) -- ISBN 978-1-61599-169-3 (ebook)
  1. Post-traumatic stress disorder--Treatment. 2. Psychic trauma--Treatment. 3.
Victims--Rehabilitation. 4. Victims of terrorism--Rehabilitation. 5. Self-esteem.
I. Title.
  RC552.P67E93 2013
  616.85'21--dc23
                          2012027988

Distributed by:
Baker & Taylor, Bertrams Books, Ingram Book Group, New Leaf Distributing

Published by:
Loving Healing Press
5145 Pontiac Trail
Ann Arbor, MI 48105
USA

http://www.LovingHealing.com or
info@LHPress.com
Tollfree 888-761-6268
Fax +1 734 663 6861

Loving Healing Press

Dedication

To: Mom, Caroline M. Ewart, who left this life July 2, 2006. And to my children: Melissa, Stephanie, Kristen, Jennifer, Alexandra, and Rebecca

Also to my clergy, faculty, and students of St. James the Elder Theological Seminary and the Holy Catholic Church International, who lovingly give me constant encouragement, comfort, and fulfillment

Plus my publisher, Victor R. Volkman, who has demonstrated great dedication from the time of my first manuscript, *AM I BAD? Recovering from Abuse*

Contents

This book shows that identity in Christ is the only way to recover personhood after the depersonalization of abuse. (Bishop Kasomo Daniel, PhD, D.Sc.)

Nihil Obstat: †Bishop Kasomo Daniel, PhD, D.Sc.
           Censor Liborum & Censor deputatus
           The Society of St. Peter and Paul Inc.
           27th May 2012 Pentecost Sunday

Imprimatur: †Bishop Kasomo Daniel, PhD, D.Sc.
           Roman Catholic Bishop
           The Prelate of the Society of St. Peter
           and Paul Inc.
           27th May 2012 Pentecost Sunday

Psychometric Instruments and Assessments

Foreword

The violence that human beings are capable of perpetrating on one another is truly astonishing in variety, complexity, and far reaching impacts, not only on the individual life, but on family, culture, and the wider world. Having worked in the helping professions of secular clinical therapy, pastoral counseling, youth and family ministry, I know all too well that human violence, darkness, and evil are real. And in this world, there is a discouraging lack of healers willing to work with these walking wounded.

The bruised, damaged, and broken are all around us, not just the ones who are obvious and come to us for help, but those standing beside us in line at the grocery store, the ones that are our kid's classmates, and even the ones beside us in the church pew. Untold, unspoken, unhealed and suffering children, teens, and adults are epidemic.

Yet human beings are also very resilient; bodies heal, negative memories get stuffed into a box, and life goes on regardless of wounds and ongoing pain. The quality of a wounded life is often hobbled by the essential changes that physical, sexual, and emotional abuse cause. Healing wounds of abuse can be a complex process, but the tools used to do so can be as simple as compassion and gentleness. Dr. Ewart 'gets it'.

There are so many causes and good works for others that we can involve ourselves in; so much that can demand out contributions of money, time, and prayer. It is popular these days for celebrities to lend their names and images to causes to increase awareness and raise need funds, and this is a good and worthy thing to do. But perhaps it is because child abuse is so prevalent (not to mention still so very hidden) that it continues to often take a back seat to other more high profile issues such as diseases or disasters. In addition, we as a culture can only stand so much pain, so much suffering, before we too, like the survivor, have to turn off a part of ourselves to cope.

People like Dr. Ewart, who dedicate their professional efforts, based in a convicted faith stance are the real workers in the fields of healing abuse survivors (read: fields of the Lord). Almost daily contact with survivors, hearing their stories, or sitting with them in their pain can, in fact, become overwhelming to the healer. Even when we are not in a healing position, those we work at to help are never far from our mind. While we need to withdraw at times to refresh and care for ourselves; to heal the wounds we receive during the healing process of survivors, those who work with survivors will always be pulled back to doing so. It is more than a professional interest, it is a mission in ministry.

One great value of human knowledge and experience is the development and improvement of the means to an end. Dr. Ewart's work in this volume represents the pairing of knowledge and direct healing experience that is rooted in several traditions of addressing and healing abuse survivors. One key area of knowledge and experience Dr. Ewart taps to inform this is spirituality. Since interpersonal abuse and trauma are so very complex and varied, varied means of approach and tools used for healing survivors is almost axiomatic. *Soul Rape*, in the title alone, conveys the weight and truth of just how deep the damages to an individual survivor can go... even to the soul. But it also goes the distance to articulate making the best use of known helping tools while innovating new approaches and tools, including spiritual understandings, to wage more effective war on the evils of abuse.

As a Pastoral Counselor, I am grateful for the open and unabashed use of spiritual and theological truths that Dr. Ewart brings to the discussion. These, of course, are the source of the effective tools of compassionate care, empathy, gentleness, and respect for self determination. The underpinnings of *Soul Rape* are an unapologetic belief and demonstration of the value of human dignity, uniqueness, the incredible preciousness of each human being, and the often unique and singular path to healing for each survivor. Since one facet of the sinful nature of child and domestic abuse is that it grows exponentially, so too do those who help to heal the survivors need to consistently grow new means of treating survivor wounds. This volume goes far to satisfy that endless goal.

W.E. Krill, Jr., M.S.P.C.
Licensed Professional Counselor

.

Introduction: Trashing What We Thought We Knew

Let's take the whole bucket of what we think we know about mental illness, turn it upside down, and start all over again. What we consider psychopathology is most often an attempt to deal with somebody else's craziness. The big problem is that there is no normal way to react to craziness.

There is no such thing as a disturbed child who is not trying to survive either outright abuse or some other absurd treatment by people who are supposed to love him. Children do not have mental illnesses that grow out of a vacuum. Their behaviors are set by the way they are cared for, not cared for, or tormented.

Abuse is the strongest form of communication there is. Child abuse is a rape of the soul. Maltreatment of a child gives him a false idea of who he is. Whether physical, sexual, or emotional, child abuse implants lies deep within the psyche, or soul, of the little boy or girl. Rather than fade with age, these lies grow as the little human grows, just like initials carved in the bark of a tree grow as does the tree. Rather than shrinking, the letters get bigger and easier to see. They are the lies that bind. They force conformity to a misconception of who we are.

In adulthood, it is of little importance whether someone has a positive self-image or a negative one, for each is a delusion. Self-image is a construct that is formed through other people's expressed opinions earlier in life, combined with the experimentation of rotating personalities during the teenage years. Teens try to find the "pretended self" that will be best accepted by the people in his life. Therefore, early opinions plus experimentation form what I term the "adopted self". Most adults believe that this flimsy concept is who they really are.

When a patient comes to me with a sense of low self-esteem, I tell him he has made a good start on grasping reality. Since the "self" is already damaged and minimized, it is easier to throw away altogether. The goal is not to have good self-esteem but to have no self-esteem. What needs to be done is to drop the whole idea of self, to take it off and drop it like an old coat.

Christianity is not a self-improvement program. It is a self-replacement program whereby the lies we have absorbed about our personhood are thrown off and replaced with a strong and joyful sense of becoming; that is, growing into the person our Creator intended. Once we have disposed of the chains of the original sin through baptism, we attain a potential that flourishes through God's glorious plan for us and our willingness to cooperate with His grace. In His Kingdom, He does not choose those who are worthy but those who are willing.

Judaism holds the same premise, that God has a plan for our life. When we discover our calling, we begin an introduction to our own soul—the real and true self already created by God since before the beginning of time.

The lies implanted by child abuse are so deeply convincing that God's intentions for His child are thwarted. It is the interference with the will of God that makes abuse not only devastating but literally evil. Blocking a soul from realizing God's love for him and from accepting divine nourishment in the form of grace is every bit as evil as murder.

The nurturing and the healing of souls are rightfully the work of the church and synagogue. Priests, rabbis, and ministers who know nothing about psychology have been short-changing their flocks. The healing of injured souls has always belonged to the medical profession and later to professional psychologists and mental-health counselors, whether or not any of these practitioners have any concept of what a soul is.

The task of pastors is to connect people to God in a life-enhancing relationship that leads to eternal life. Our pastors may or may not be well-steeped in the study of divinity; that is, theology. But they are ignorant about the nature of people; that is, psychology. There exists an abyss between the two fields of knowledge.

Some seminaries do include a course or two in pastoral counseling in their basic curriculum, preparing students for ordination; but the subject matter has little depth. A pastor should at least be able to recognize when a member of his church has a mental disorder that requires expert treatment, and he should know how to conduct a group therapy session.

Well-educated and experienced mental-health professionals will always be needed by society, as will knowledgeable pastors. The point is that there is much knowledge to be shared between the two.

The lies implanted by child abusers are so deeply convincing that God's intentions for His child are thwarted. It is the interference with the will of God that makes abuse not only devastating but literally evil. Blocking a soul from realizing God's love for him and from accepting divine nourishment in the form of grace is every bit as evil as murder.

Child abuse and domestic violence are a dual pandemic. They are linked, for the first leads to the second, in my experience. Many professionals are surprised at this observation, but I have attempted to show the connection in this volume. An abused child becomes prone to abuse in adulthood. Although both subjects have been extensively studied, much of the literature deals only with a description of each. Rarely are they discussed together. Moreover, existing documentation tends only to describe in general how horrible child abuse is, both in degree and in frequency, and how hopeless the struggle of society is to stop domestic violence from continuing to skyrocket. Stopping domestic violence altogether has received little scholarly attention.

The literature is thus replete with accounts of what is happening in our culture, but little has been written about why. One of the most important factors in domestic violence has been overlooked in research and in practice; that is, the treatment of the affliction. Too often, shelters provide a haven for a time; but when the victim is released, she either returns to the same abuser or seeks out a worse one. Not only is the cycle not broken, but the victim becomes even more vulnerable.

The purpose of this book is to provide from real-life case histories a penetrating and hopefully unforgettable look at the murderous nature of child abuse. Vivid understanding of what abuse does to the soul must precede the development of effective treatment. Further, the intent is to show the destruction of the sense of self, which greatly limits the chances of a fulfilling life. Child abuse implants false messages about who one is. It is most difficult to live a successful life that is based on lies.

When clinicians and others with the power to produce change really see what child abuse does, the adult ramifications of this phenomenon, including domestic violence, can be treated with greater success.

<table>
<tr><td>1</td><td># Disintegration of Life</td></tr>
</table>

Pretty little Amy, only nine years old, was playing near her inner-city home when a stranger raped her in full view of her young friends. Worse than the assault was her father's condemnation that placed full blame on her for letting it happen, and the onset of rejection. His words, "It's your own fault," formed an unceremonious branding of the child as a "less-than" that would be confirmed by periodic acts of sexual assaults against her as time went on. Each subsequent violation of her personhood was committed by people who were supposed to love her, not by strangers.

The stranger assaulted her body, shamed her beyond words, and made her feel like a piece of trash. But her own father is the one who raped her soul. He denied her the chance to form even an "adopted self". She was left without a clue as to her own existence. *She ceased to exist.*

By the time she entered her teen years, the original Amy was gone. There remained the form of a maturing female who knew no power of her own except for the ability to gain attention and meet survival needs through the sexual use of her body. So she sold it in order to exist. When she discovered that crack cocaine worked miraculously to lift her away from the anguish of nonexistence, she became a loyal slave to it.

She was only in her late teens when her body would no longer bring enough money for both living and crack. So she sold her body for crack only. She came down with pneumonia, and while in the hospital, she was diagnosed with AIDS. It was found that that she had carried the virus for a very long time. She estimated that she might have infected more than 150 men. Even while she was hospitalized, with oxygen at her nose and a feeding tube in her throat, and intravenous lines in her veins, she continued to accept the clients who came to her hospital room for their usual service. She lived almost two years after the first hospitalization, but because her lifestyle remained unchanged, she was dead by 24. Upon physically dying, she entered eternal life and came to know the unspeakable joy of real love for the first time. Only through death did she attain a life. Even though child abuse crosses all economic lines, poverty is the most prominent cause of child maltreatment. (Pelton, 2011)

Larry – Growing up Abused

Larry was neglected in foster homes from birth to age 2, when the real trouble began. His adoptive father hated him. He was yelled at, beaten, thrown out to agencies, brought back, cursed, ignored, insulted, and belittled until he was farmed out permanently to a boys' home in his early teens. His adoptive mother, living in terror that her husband might kill both of them, kept her mouth shut and even continued living with the man long after the boy had grown up.

Such is usually the case with mother figures living with a predator. She stands by and witnesses the step-by-step destruction of her child in order to hang on to her "man". Many mothers even become jealous of the attention the child receives, no matter how brutal. In other cases, they directly blame a sexually violated child by openly accusing the child of seduction.

The young man never told anyone but his therapist that when he was four, he used to wake up from nightmares about something hard and slimy under his blanket. When he awoke and felt the mattress, he wondered where the substance came from and what it was.

All of his life, he was tormented by his uncertain sexual identity. Even as this book was being written, he wondered whether he was bi-sexual or homosexual. But there is one thing he knew for sure: He was dying of full-blown AIDS, and in his mind, it was his rightful punishment for causing his father to hate him. Larry died before this book was published.

He had lived in a single room in a 10-story subsidized housing facility. Long abandoned by his family, he had no visitors, except for me, his support-counseling advisor. I recall him always sweating profusely with the air conditioner on high, full-blast, even in winter. I had to keep my coat on when I was in his apartment.

Most of all, I remember how he would beam each time he saw me, even though it was only one hour once a week. My job was only to provide company, but I treated him anyway, with the goal of freeing him from guilt. Most importantly, I did help him accept that he was a child of God with as much value as anyone and that his abuse was caused by the abuser, not by him, the victim.

Eventually, another therapist, a man, took my place and after about a month, made a pass at him. Larry was so upset by the incident that he called the agency providing the service and cancelled any future "therapy".

St. Paul called the love of money the root of all kinds of evil. But child abuse is an evil root that runs deeper, spreads farther, and holds a specific, predictable consequence: the loss of personhood and often of life itself.

Always feeling despicable, the victim has neither hope nor any concept of eternal life. There is no possibility of a healthy relationship with God.

While AIDS is only one example, it is a recurring demonstration of abuse leading to a deadly disease. When a mind is set off course, the body follows.

In 2004, I presented a continuing education class on domestic violence for a medical center in Jacksonville, Florida. I began my remarks with this statement: "Domestic violence begins at age four." Abuse at the hands of a partner in early adulthood does not arise out of a vacuum merely by the poor choice of a mate. Rather, maltreatment from this stage on is very often the natural outcome of a type of "brainwashing" that begins early and receives reinforcement many times through the years.

It is during the early years that humans acquire their first ideas about who they are, and, unfortunately, they believe these falsehoods for the rest of their lives. Victims are initiated into a pattern of abuse, including self-abuse, not in adulthood, but in childhood. As a matter of fact, every one of us comes into adulthood with a second-hand opinion of who we are.

When a little child is called brilliant, stupid, beautiful, ugly, hopeless, helpless, good, bad, a blessing, or a curse, the child has no choice but to accept these assertions as "gospel". What other source of information does he have? He can absorb only the information available to him.

These messages are communicated just as well or better by what is unsaid. The glances, the pauses, the scowls, the smiles, the visual forces, all speak indelibly, although without sound. The child's self-definition derives from these impressions. They are permanent, like initials carved in the bark of a young tree that only enlarge as the tree grows.

You may have wondered by now why an example of male abuse has been included in our opening case histories, when little girls are abused, especially sexually, far more often. The reason is that the effects are the same. Female sexual abuse is slightly more prevalent. As best we know, one in every three little girls is sexually abused and about one in four boys. There is no way to know the actual prevalence because, of course, abuse occurs in secret. However, it is fairly accurate to say that perhaps 90 percent of women attending Alcoholics Anonymous have been sexually abused, and about 80 percent of the men have been physically abused, a large but unknown number sexually. Half the abused women are victims of incest. Present studies indicate about 40 million children abused per day world-wide.

When the child reaches adolescence, having mastered the lessons about who he is, he is driven to experiment. His concept of self may not work in the peer group, so various trial personalities and their accompanying behavior must be rotated until one works. Not to fit in means annihilation, not just rejection, and today the consequences can mean physical attacks as well. Clothes with the wrong label might literally be torn from his back.

In adulthood, the urgency to meet life on its own terms, that is, deal with the challenges of living, becomes more pressing, with countless choices to be made. One's identity, or a solid sense of who one is, determines the direction of these choices. But this idea of "self" is no more than a chance configuration. It is formed by combining the second-hand opinions received in childhood with the results of adolescent experimentation. Victims enter adult life with the greatest possible handicap—believing they know who they are and being wrong, or, alternatively, having no idea whatsoever. Either case requires dependence on someone else.

While child abuse might harshly be stated as "raping the soul", even children reared in fairly normal homes still suffer a "molestation" of their identity through the communication of false information about themselves. The messages can even be seemingly positive. I have met nearly-retarded people who were told all of their lives that they were brilliant, and the result was a life of endless frustration as they attempted to achieve goals that were impossible for them. And worse, they left unattended great possibilities in other realms that would have paid off with great enrichment.

But the tragedies I have seen over 28 years of practice mostly result from destructive, even malicious, assertions about the child's nature on the part of parents, teachers, siblings, and other influential members of the child's early social circle. This "programming" has cheated them out of a fulfilling life that could have fostered the greatest joy of all: being and celebrating their own self, a completely unique creation of God Himself. Indeed, for those who are spiritual, blossoming into the fullness of one's being—with the hidden talents, gifts, and abilities thoroughly explored—is the highest honor to one's Creator, however that divine entity may be defined. It might even be argued that such is the highest form of praise. One victim who responded very well to treatment proclaimed:

> For the first time in my life, I have been given the greatest sense of freedom: to know that the career I have chosen, that of a dedicated mother and wife, reflects the real 'me' and therefore is honorable, is a huge joy. I don't have to listen to the old messages, that I'm no good, that I'm bad.
>
> I have spent my whole life feeling like a worthless piece of *sh*—. No matter how hard I tried, my father and step-mother would always put me down. I could do nothing to make them happy, to accept me. I could not make them give me the affection and feeling of worth I always needed so badly.

I'm not to blame for their inabilities as parents. I'm learning that I didn't cause their unhappiness, that the messages I was given as a child were false.

I have always believed bad things happened because I was a bad girl; that I was unworthy to have a mother; that it was my fault that a neighbor molested me—my fault because I was the one who went into his house.

I have let people abuse me verbally and physically because I believed that is what I deserved. Today, I'm learning I don't deserve to be treated that way. I am finding myself, my true self!

There is hope for people like me, and I believe if doctors become aware of what child abuse does, people like me can recover instead of being misdiagnosed, institutionalized, given improper medications, and ending up suicidal.

The Statistical Evidence

From the American Professional Society on the Abuse of Children, perhaps the most reliable authority today[1]:

Perpetrator Relationship

Victim data were analyzed by relationship of duplicate victims to their perpetrators. Four-fifths (81.3%) of victims were maltreated by a parent either acting alone or with someone else. Nearly two-fifths (37.2%) of victims were maltreated by their mother acting alone. One-fifth (19.1%) of victims were maltreated by their father acting alone. One-fifth (18.5%) of victims were maltreated by both parents. Thirteen percent of victims were maltreated by a perpetrator who was not a parent of the child. (See table 3–10.)

Child Victim Demographics

The remaining analyses in this chapter focus on the demographics of the child victims and were conducted using the unique count of victims. The youngest children are the most vulnerable to maltreatment. More than one-third (34.0%) of all FFY 2010 unique victims were younger than 4 years. One-fifth (23.4%) of victims were in the age group 4–7 years. (See table 3–11, figure 3–4, and related notes.)

Children younger than 1 year had the highest rate of victimization at 20.6 per 1,000 children in the population of the

---

[1] http://www.acf.hhs.gov/programs/cb/pubs/cm09/cm09.pdf

same age. Victims with the single-year age of 1, 2, or 3 years old had victimization rates of 11.9, 11.4, and 11.0 victims per 1,000 children of those respective ages in the population. In general, the rate and percentage of victimization decreased with age.

Victimization was split between the sexes, with boys accounting for 48.5 percent and girls accounting for 51.2 percent. Fewer than 1 percent of victims had an unknown sex. (See table 3–12 and related notes.)

Eighty-eight percent of unique victims were comprised of three races or ethnicities—African-American (21.9%), Hispanic (21.4%), and White (44.8%). However, victims of African-American, American-Indian or Alaska Native, and multiple racial descents had the highest rates of victimization at 14.6, 11.0, and 12.7 victims, respectively, per 1,000 children in the population of the same race or ethnicity. (See table 3–13, figure 3–5, and related notes.)

As far back as 1997, 41 states reported that nearly 1,000 children were known by child protective agencies to have died as a result of abuse or neglect in each state reporting. These agencies further estimated reports of physical abuse at the 3-million mark nationwide, but admit that a high but unknown percentage of cases are never reported. (U.S. Dept. Health and Human Services, 1997).

Recent statistics are even more staggering, as illustrated by one single state, South Carolina. The website Childwelfare.com, hosted by Duncan Lindsey, indicates a child population of 1,009,641, with 11,246 of these children abused in 2002 alone. (This is a national site, where your own state can be examined.) Nationally, this source reports the highest percentage of abuse to occur in the 0 to 3 age group (16%), followed by 4 to 7 (13.7 %), then 8 to 11 (11.9%), 12 to 15 (10.6%), and 16 to 17 (6.0%).

But as serious as these abuses are, they do not match the greatest damage: the message that abuse implants in the child permanently.

Another patient reports:

> I used to have images cross my mind, then quickly dismiss them. I had no reason to believe anything like sexual abuse had happened to me. After all, no one in my family had said anything tragic had happened to me or my family when I was four years old.
>
> My pain escalated in adulthood until I was brave enough to consider that something had happened and gave myself permission to explore the idea. I was like a computer unable to

proceed until the sequence was right. I've learned to pay attention to these images—that is, flashbacks—sometimes visual, sometimes almost audible, all packed with feelings.

My molestation was filled with emotional messages which I have believed for 43 years. My assailant was my "true love". "Don't tell anyone. They won't like you," he said. These messages were recalled only by my being in a group. While others were sharing, little pieces of my own life started to come together.

It has been a lot of painstaking emotional pain to discover all this, but it's been worth it, to be able to proceed with my life. Now, at 43, I am finally rid of the garbage and am reasonably happy.

When my molester almost got caught, he abandoned me, and left me feeling false guilt: that it was my fault. To make matters worse, I was a victim of a dysfunctional, negative, and abusive family that fed on my weakness. I was the oldest of seven children and was told how to feel, how not to feel, so I believed I had no right to my own feelings. That apparently made it harder to discover what I do feel and to trust those feelings as cues to my recovery. I couldn't do anything fast enough or well enough to meet their approval, adding to my distress.

The weather even had an effect on me. The sun casting a certain shadow triggered deep emotional feelings of fear, sadness, and aloneness. The same with certain sounds and music. I am learning to pay attention to these things, to recognize them and deal with them and get healthy.

Too few professionals are up to date on what they need to know about the devastation of child abuse. The American Professional Society on the Abuse of Children (APSAC), an organization I highly value and depend upon, conducted a survey of professional needs (APSAC, 1994) and confirmed that competent assistance for victims is a literal void.

There is simply not enough competent help for abuse victims. Interdisciplinary people working in the field cited as the most difficult aspects of their work, "Heavy workload, low pay, public laws and policies that impede my work, and lack of communication with interdisciplinary colleagues."

One woman believes she would not have survived if she had not found our therapy group. A psychiatric nurse as well as a survivor of child and domestic abuse, she says our understanding and treatment go far beyond what is now being offered in the field at large:

They have given me an understanding of the trauma, so
that I can live with it, on a daily basis. Healing from trauma
takes time, understanding, encouragement, and compassion
that few professionals are willing or able to give, in my
experience. My doctor has been gifted in this field. He has
saved my life and given me a sense of peace within that I have
searched for in a therapist for years. The ideas he presents make
sense and give people hope that they can overcome the trauma
that has been inflicted on them.

APSAC reports that child protective agencies nationally were able to
investigate only 28 percent of cases in which children were harmed by
maltreatment in 1993, compared with 44 percent in 1986. It is
acknowledged that these facts are far from recent, but research has always
been a low priority compared with other national health issues.

An anonymous, inner-city teacher, writing in the Society's booklet,
"Connecting with Kids," reports,

I see a lot of this kind of thing [child abuse], but D was one
of the most troubling kids I'd seen. At seven years of age, he
was fatalistic, foul-mouthed, and jumpy. He was
hypervigilant—he seemed scared all the time, and he was
utterly unable to concentrate. You'd see a flash of sweetness in
him now and then, but mostly he was too on-guard for that.

The day he came in with a welt on his cheek, I decided it
was time to call child protective services. The caseworker
hooked up with the police to do a home visit, where they found
total chaos—filth, rotating boyfriends, violence among the
adults, violence in the neighborhood. Both the mom and several
of her boyfriends had been in and out of prison. Mom had dealt
some drugs. Years ago, people would have said that D was a
"troublemaker"; now we say he's a kid suffering from post-
traumatic stress disorder as a result of violence in his home and
neighborhood. (APSAC Advisor).

Post-traumatic stress disorder (PTSD) is one of the more easily definable
outcomes of child abuse. Most severely victimized children, in my
experience, can be accurately diagnosed for PTSD. Not until adulthood,
when life stresses compound, do they eventually seek treatment; that is,
those few who do. As for the children, they are often diagnosed with
hyperactivity, attention-deficit disorder, conduct disorder, Asperger's
syndrome, and even bi-polar disorder. Notice that the victim always gets the
label, never the abuser.

Most traumatized people abuse alcohol and other drugs. They are found everywhere in Twelve-Step programs including Alcoholics Anonymous, Overeaters Anonymous, and Narcotics Anonymous meetings. Current estimates of the number of female incest survivors in Twelve-Step programs. range from 40 to 80 percent. Similarly, about an equal percentage of men in these groups have survived some sort of physical abuse as children, according to many studies (AA World Services, 2012). Nearly 100 percent of these victims have never been treated. Those who relapse the most—or completely give up—tend to be those who have been through the worst nightmares that life has to offer children.

The public at large seems to blame the male homosexual for the AIDS epidemic. However, the group spreading the disease most rapidly today consists of intravenous drug abusers. Many of them, perhaps easily the majority, were pointed toward the needle not by the peer group but by the abuse in childhood. Perhaps some make it all the way to elementary school before their true selves are mangled. But one thing is sure in my experience: Rarely does a substance abuser know who he is.

2 | The Recovering of Self

A New Developmental Model

The average reader is likely familiar with the established models of personality development. For example, one school, espoused by Rothbart (1988) and Kagan (Kaplan, 1993, 1989) link inborn temperament to adjustment in later life. Freud sees development as progressing through a series of psychosexual stages (FreudNet, 1996). Erickson (Ames, 1993) was the first to stress social factors in personality formation, and he emphasized such concepts as trust versus mistrust and identity versus role confusion.

Levinson (1986) divided the lifespan into transitional stages and introduced the concept of "midlife crisis". Baumrind (1991) saw styles of parenting as important factors in personality formation.

It can readily be seen that the more recent theorists progress toward a realization of interpersonal events as major factors directing the course of maturation from infancy to adulthood. They are getting closer to the truth. I, however, take a much different approach. Instead of describing how children might ideally develop, I propose a model based on what I have seen as a clinician, treating most known forms of emotional distress and crippling mental disorders for 28 years. My premise is that all children, to some degree, absorb erroneous information about themselves that can misdirect their course through life, prevent full maturation—no matter what model is used to measure, and create a false identity. I have named this the "adopted self". This adopted self can work rather successfully when a child has been fortunate in his life experiences, although it is not the "real self". Children who are "lied to" about their nature are destined to acquire an adopted self that limits life in direct proportion to the severity of the false information. Child abuse is the worst case, where the most severe lies are communicated most often and most forcefully.

As mentioned briefly in Chapter 1, all people cross the line from childhood to adulthood with a secondhand opinion of who they are.

Without any questioning, we take as truth whatever our parents and other influentials have said about us during our formative years, whether those messages are communicated verbally, physically, or silently.

Children have two basic vulnerabilities that directly pertain to this model. One, they are gullible, and two, their sources of information are limited. They must depend on whatever information is available to form a concept of self.

Similarly, even parents who are capable and who would be considered loving are not perfect. Thus, even the best-intentioned parent cannot, without a flaw, consistently convey the truth about a child to that child. The only source for the truth about an identity is God.

These impressions, accumulated by the child, then later combined with an idea of what the world will accept, form most of the construct of self image. No matter how absurdly false, these early impressions are the ones that register deeply and permanently, and that we automatically accept as true to a very large extent. Even those experiences we vividly remember, wherein we rejected an accusation or railed against some falsehood asserted against us, have their penetrating and lasting impact because we do not totally disbelieve them.

The adopted self is the personal image we use to operate in adult life. It should be self-evident that there is a "true self" that exists somewhere, that we were born with, and that forms the substance of who we are in fact. There must be some way that this true self can be accessed. It can be, and that method is discussed later in the chapter on treatment considerations. But let it be said right here that the discovery of the true self is the successful outcome of therapy for many of the most common psychological disorders. This is the "pearl of great price," whose uncovering should be the goal in the treatment of most conditions.

In common with other models of development, the adopted self progresses through a series of stages. These milestones are measured in terms of power acquisition, experimentation, and ingesting the impressions formed during these processes. Of great importance is the internal impact of information communicated about one's self through the process.

I postulate (see Table 2-1 on p. 13) that the true self, which many religions regard as the "soul", is fully expressed from before birth to about age two. But abuse and neglect can stifle this freedom. At age two, the child is able to attach significant meaning to the messages of others. Also, in this age period, there is no sense of power but only of freedom to act.

From age 2 to 6, the self is modified, but not substantially changed, by required and forbidden behaviors that have consequences determined by the caregiver. During this stage, there is imagined power, and in fact, the imagination plays a major role in self-determination. The greater the imagination, the greater the range of choices for thought material later in life.

By age 6, and continuing up to the edge of adolescence, the self becomes subordinated to both opinion and experience. It is in this period that claims or comments are made by others as to the character, worth, and abilities of the child, which the child internalizes.

Of course, the interaction with parents or parental surrogates has the greatest influence. When a father or mother is especially forceful, or in some way very effective, in what is said about the child, the impression is more difficult to remove—as if the information becomes encapsulated or "wired into" the developing soul, forever protected and able to become more influential, not less, as time passes. This "capsule" is more active in adulthood than in childhood. A great-grandmother will recite her capsule as readily as a newlywed.

	Womb to 2	Age 2-6	Age 6-13	Adolescence
Development of adopted self	True self dominates	Self molded	Self altered	Trial selves rotate
Power	No power	Imaginary power	Pretended power	Struggle for power
Freedom	No freedom	Loss of freedom	Pretended Freedom	Struggle for freedom
Messages	Receptive to	Resisted	Receptive again	Struggle to reject

Table 2-1: Formation of the Adopted Self

Also in this stage (age 6-13), there is "pretended power", as opposed to imaginary power. Here is when you see young boys tying towels around their shoulders and jumping out of trees as though they could fly like superman. In addition, severely maltreated children will form ideas of their revenge, which they increasingly are prone to carry out. It is easy for a parent to begin making a murderer, and many parents do. A delinquent is not a child *turned* bad but rather one who is formed to commit sociopathic behavior.

Even conscientious, loving parents fail to examine the accuracy or timing of the messages they give. Besides what is said outright, parents and other intimates communicate just as deeply by what they do not say—even by facial expressions by which a father may strike terror in the heart of his young son or daughter. Day after day, the identity is being formed, malformed, or misformed. Abuse or neglect at this stage, as we shall see later, often mangles any truth the child may have obtained about himself. Even the opportunity to develop an adopted self is denied.

Good parents, without knowing, have their own agenda, at least sometimes, when they make remarks about the child. Such exclamations as "You're just like your father," for example, say nothing about the child but everything about the parent. In addressing their children, parents vent their own misconceptions, hopes, fears, confusion, and doubts. They unknowingly reveal their own adopted self when they try to describe their child.

This is an appropriate place to point out a very great tragedy, which grown sons and daughters increasingly must accept at some stage. While virtually all children love their parents unconditionally, not all parents love their children.

When a child is maliciously denied access to his real personhood, he is doomed to spend his life in a trial-and-error process of discovery in which every piece of evidence is questionable. This choice and the acceptance of the lies as truth are the only alternatives. He is likely to join a violent gang or perhaps an exclusive clique that denies membership to inferior people.

Again referring to Table 2-1 (p. 13), the adolescent carries but a remnant of the true self of infancy. He may believe his accumulation of messages or he may reject them, but he is not certain either way. He doesn't know who he is or who he wants to be. Besides this fact, acceptance by the peer group becomes paramount. At the very time when the child most needs his parents, he will have nothing to do with their beliefs and will sever himself from family ties to some extent—often as completely as possible.

The adolescent must somehow gather the strength to experiment with various trial "personalities" in order to find one that is suitable for the peer group he thinks he should belong to. A maltreated child will not be up to this enormously challenging task and will develop symptoms. He will drop out. He will get into rebellion, very often including drug or alcohol abuse. Others, not as badly treated, will give the process a try but not succeed. They fail to find a combination that works, and thus they are rejected by the group. Such an outcome introduces a "less-than" mentality with which to enter adulthood.

Survival Needs

A critically important factor added to this new developmental model is the concept of survival needs.

It is my assertion that the needs of the child are the needs of the adult. That is, needs do not change, and they do not go away. Even when needs are met, they remain to be fulfilled again and again. When not met, they will scream out in the form of behavioral, affective, cognitive, or personality disorders, either episodically or chronically. The most important need in the maturation process at any stage is affirmation of the true self, the soul.

Parents who teach their children to be agnostic or atheistic do not free them from superstition; they rob them of an identity given by God and the security of knowing that a loving Creator will always offer protection—also that there is meaning in suffering.

Several of the extant models, such as those of Piaget and Erickson, emphasize needs in childhood. But the reason that needs are permanent throughout life is that they arise from the true self, from the child within us all. The adopted self of adulthood is not the real person but only an artificial construct. The true self is the one who comes directly from the womb but who exists long before birth because the Father has so willed.

Correct verbal and nonverbal messages on the part of parents are always crucial, even in adolescence. A boy needs a father, and a girl needs a mother, just as much as in earlier stages. A father who has suffered neglect or rejection by his own father will not only be hampered but often utterly crippled in his ability to be open, approachable, and affectionate, especially to a son.

The effect of an inadequate father, whether neglectful or demanding, is never less than devastating to the son's personhood. The son is prevented from having a full sense of being a male. Father is the one who grants the "rite of passage" to manhood, and he is also the one who can block it. If the boy sees no hand extended and hears no voice saying in some way, "Welcome to manhood," he never fully "arrives" in his own mind but carries the sense of being more boy than man all his life.

A daughter denied affirmation by a father lives out her whole life with a sense of not completely existing. The lives of such unfortunates are continuous efforts to stave off the fear of annihilation—worse than the fear of death. Feeling as though one doesn't exist is more terrifying than the knowledge that one will someday die.

Daughters go to extremes to counteract this bottomless deficit. They will take a tyrannical father and make him, in their own fantasies, a sweet, wonderful man. Or they will search for their "real father" in relationship after relationship, never realizing whom they are really leaving each time they break from a partner. They will fight their own buried conviction that they must indeed be loathsome if "My own father couldn't love me," and they will invariably project these voids and fears onto their concept of God.

Sometimes they will sell their bodies with the meager comfort of feeling that "I must be worth something if men will pay money for me." A similar phenomenon can be seen in the ambitious model or actress who endlessly pursues some important person to "take my picture." The personal account of one of my own recent patients graphically illustrates the point:

> I married at 17, was a virgin, and wanted to leave home. I rationalized a lot, you see. I prided myself in the fact that I

stayed a virgin, although my parents were very strict. I married the first man I dated. I got pregnant on my honeymoon.

When my husband later beat me and my 3-month-old daughter, I divorced him. My dad moved me and my daughter back home. The second man I had sex with looked surprised when I asked him if he was going to hurt me, and he said, "No." What I meant to ask was whether he was going to hurt me emotionally, and he did. All I meant to him was sex.

The one thing I was proud of, being a virgin, was long gone. So I rationalized that this was the cause of my increasing promiscuity. I was good at rationalizing. I made up my own philosophies, and then would change them or add to them to make some sense of the deep emotional wounds with a tremendous amount of pain. My parents were too strict. I regretted ever being such a good girl. Why didn't I go ahead and just have sex before marriage? After all, I probably wouldn't have ended up beaten and I wouldn't have had the silly dreams that I could actually be happily married or just plain old happy. It wasn't until recently that I found out that I was set up for all of this from the age of 4.

My mom was physically and verbally abused when she was growing up, and her dad was alcoholic. My dad was an alcoholic from a divorced home, and both of his parents were killed by automobiles when my dad was very young, around 11 or 12. He lived with his mom's parents after his mom and dad divorced when he was about 7. His mom moved 300 miles away to find work and didn't see him often, but made sure he was well-dressed.

Dad had a sister who was diagnosed as schizophrenic in her 40s, after she cursed out the phone company and served time in prison for it. That's almost all I know about my parents' histories. Dad doesn't talk much about his family. He is a very emotional man but emotionally unavailable to me.

That brings me to the remembrance of one of the many times he hurt my feelings and one of my brothers came out to comfort me. He told me I had to understand my dad was a drill sergeant and a military policeman in the Army. His way of treating me was to make me tough. I didn't buy it then, and I still don't buy it now; nor do I excuse it. This thing runs in families, you know. This is a dysfunction, if you haven't guessed yet.

There was a lot of verbal and physical abuse from my parents. But no matter how bad it was, my mother's reply was that our life was never as bad as what she had to endure growing up. "I did the best I could, and I treated all you kids the same," she would say. "I don't think I did too bad when I was raising you kids, and I wouldn't have anyone but your dad. He's the only man for me." All this when I know different.

My dad's responses, behavior, and attitude were always— and I mean always—negative; except, of course, when it came to babies. He had seven of us, and he could handle babies. He loved babies. But when each of us became about 5 years old, the distance began. I know. I watched it happen.

I was the oldest of us seven. It was, most of the time, "It's too hot," or "It's too cold." "You're stupid." "That's stupid." "What's wrong with you?" "Your hair looks like sh—." "You should know better." "You always have your head up your a-- ." Etc., etc., and then… total indifference.

It was, and still is, impossible to get any warmth from him, and I really tried all my life. About one and a half years ago, I really thought I had caught on to something when, at the funeral of my 19-year-old nephew, I was really hurting from seeing him in the casket for the first time, and I held onto my daddy and asked him to tell me he loved me. And he did, and even patted me gently on the back and gave me a hug.

The first time I called to chat after that, I ended the conversation with "I love you." And he said, "I love you." I really thought things had changed. I was so happy. The next time I called I ended with "I love you," and the response was, "yeah."

In late adolescence, the young person begins for the first time to consider the future and begins to look at various occupations. The choice of the way to make a living is restricted to "no more than I deserve," just as the choice of a partner is limited by the same measure. A woman marries a man who is no better than what she thinks she deserves. She is not surprised at all when the abuse begins to develop in the relationship. She will make excuses for him no matter how atrocious the abuse becomes, even when he repeatedly nearly kills her.

Many daughters are brought up with the unspoken message that their job for life is to serve Mother. A mother companion can be guaranteed success by convincing the daughter from the earliest time that there is something not quite right about her (the child) and that she can never make it on her own. Some mothers, who are particularly malicious, will force the little girl to believe she is mentally ill.

A lady I am presently treating was put in a psychiatric hospital when she was seven years old. Now in her early 40s, she doubts her own sanity frequently because her mother sees to it daily, either by phone or in-person. But therapy has been highly successful. This patient now needs only to call me several times a week for a minute or two of reassurance. But in the beginning, my job was very difficult because her mother's lies were driven in so forcefully and substantiated by psychiatrists and a parade of other mental-health professionals through the years, right up to the present. The other day, this dear woman texted me and apologized for not calling because she was too busy.

Mothers who place little value on their daughters' lives, compared to their own, can have a servant for life by always being unhappy and never letting the daughter please her fully. There was once in my care a 67-year-old woman who 40 years previously had divorced her husband in favor of coming back to Mother. Mother, now 93, was still not pleased at all with her daughter, who complained during one session, "Dr. Ewart, my mother treats me like a little girl. I'm not a little girl. I'm a big girl." Then Mother shot back, "Then act like one!"

This daughter was a retired director of nursing at a major medical center. In her professional career, she enjoyed the highest respect and recognition of her colleagues. But none of them had designs on her as a servant.

The same tragic "game" can play between a mother and her son. Never having gotten her needs met through her husband, she turns to her son for emotional support. Some young men—and some not so young—find that drug or alcohol abuse provides justification for never leaving home. It is more face-saving to be home due to addictive disease than to be there because you can't leave your mother.

Some men go to another extreme: having an extramarital affair in order to destroy the marriage, after which they can go home. Such men have then been able to say that the marriage was destroyed by an affair rather than the primary need to go home. The same happens with women. In fact, one of the main causes of infidelity in my experience is the need to go back home. Often I can quickly determine the cause of the breakup by watching where the partners go once the marriage is over. Husbands and wives have been shocked to discover in therapy that it wasn't a sexual tryst that did them in, but in fact, an emotional affair with a parent.

Having come through the emotion-charged personality experiments of adolescence, the adult's sense of identity is now an adopted self, a culmination of earlier opinions plus the trial and error of the teens. It is this adopted self that governs the adult, with the result that very few individuals ever take a look back and question the messages of childhood. Most people go to their graves without an accurate idea of who they are or who they should have become; they never stopped to ask God why He put them here.

The Sense of Becoming

The "sense of becoming" is related to the perception of power discussed earlier. A sense of "being" and of having power are required in order to stave off the fear of annihilation, the greatest of all fears that mankind retains. A sense of becoming fosters the substance of being, and with being comes power. The greater the sense of being, the greater the sense of power to resist the fear of annihilation, that threatens at all times to penetrate into full consciousness. This fear is so basic and so horrible, far exceeding the fear of death, that it is not faced by mankind.

But how does one come to be and thus gain the power for living? Victor Frankl asserts that all of mankind is searching for the meaning of life and that this meaning is a primary ingredient for the survival of personhood (Frankl, 1998). Abraham Maslow sees "self actualization" as the desired outcome in his developmental model, an exciting concept that formed the basis for the "Human Potential Movement" (Cerny, 1996).

Maslow believed that if the environment is right, people grow straight and beautiful, actualizing the potentials they have inherited. Such a premise somewhat resembles my own experience in practice. However, he said the only reason that people would not move well in the direction of self-actualization is that hindrances are placed in the way by society, primarily the educational system. I would include the educational system, but the process of derailment begins in the pre-school years and is powered more by parents than by teachers.

Eric Erickson points to such holdbacks as shame and doubt, guilt, role confusion, and despair (Kottler and Brown, 1992). Conversely, he believes trust, autonomy, initiative, industry, identity, intimacy, generativity, and integrity to be the markers of successful development. Such qualities cannot be denied as measures of maturity; however, arriving at these levels is an ideal that few achieve. Late maturity, he postulates, brings the realization of wisdom and a period of reflection about life or the regret over lost opportunity. On this last point, we are in absolute agreement.

Many have considered the words, "what might have been" the saddest in human experience. The popular duo Simon and Garfunkel sing, "A bad day is when I lie in bed and think of what might have been."

According to my experience, discovering one's "mission" in life helps describe more than anything else who one really is. While Christians might refer to the concept as a "calling", and others may term it "destiny", it is essential that every individual have a sense of having a life purpose, whether of value to one's creator (if such a belief is held), to society, or simply one's self. For many, the purpose of becoming can be the mere capacity to enjoy life fully by discovering and then celebrating who they are.

If one compares the brain to a computer, as in artificial intelligence, the slogan of programmers, "garbage in, garbage out," is illustrative. It can be seen that the human mind, when inaccurately "programmed", produces thinking and reacting that consist of "cognitive malfunctions". It might be crudely said that the brain that registers false information has a "software" problem.

Some, and perhaps many, forms of mental illness, whether a simple adjustment disorder or deep, chronic mental illness of major proportions, originate with a skewed or totally false sense of self. It is the mislearning during the developmental years that leads to psychopathology in many cases. The reason is that the adopted self, operating on false information, has too little power to stand up to the challenges of life or to maintain orderly direction.

Now, before the critics begin to pounce, let me say clearly that my premise applies to "many" psychological disorders, not to "all." Human beings are far too complicated to explain in terms of any one theory. Further, as psychology continues to take its place among the recognized sciences, having long-ago graduated from being mere philosophy, genuine research in countless areas will provide ongoing information about the human psyche and the interrelatedness between body and mind.

What I do mean to say is that the acquisition of misinformation has been largely overlooked in the etiology of mental illness and therefore should be included as an exploration that could provide a major contribution to personality theory and psychopathology. There is some precedent in the "cognitive psychology" of Beck and Ellis. Ellis's false beliefs and Beck's core beliefs dovetail with this idea.

Moving back to our model of development, we can see that an infant has no sense of becoming; that is, no sense of the development of self. From age 2 to 6, however, the child explores the world of fantasy, an unbridled journey into activities, wishes, and imaginings that are not preemptively censored by naysaying adults. Here we see the true self fully expressed in thousands of ways. Through all this activity of mind and body, the child celebrates an unrestricted being. There are no limits in the beginning period of this stage of development, and only few limits all the way to the end of this stage. This period holds the primary clues as to who the person is. The child, during this age period, and the preceding, is the true self.

These stages, however, are highly vulnerable. Abuse at this time has more devastating consequences than at any other, because the self is fully exposed, without protection. The self is open to receiving all information through sensation and through words.

While the infant has no sense of power, the young child acquires a "taste" of power as he experiences how people, objects, and his own body respond to his own will. This taste leads to a "sense" of power.

The sense of power extends into the next stage, 6 to 13, where power must be constrained through outside influences; for example, discipline. But the child, while forced to submit to restrictions, maintains his belief that his power is unlimited; hence, the "illusion of power". It is here that we see little boys jumping out of trees to fly as superman. They continue to imagine, no matter how many times they fall to the ground, that a jump is coming that will lead to flight.

Boys dream of becoming firemen, doctors, policemen, and karate champions. Girls "know" they will be a princess, a model, or a ballerina, when they grow up. Anything and everything is possible. But as children progress through this stage, their joy of becoming increasingly fades as outside influence competes with their illusion of power and eventually wins, though only partially.

In adolescence, about age 14 to 18, and perhaps beyond, the illusion of power has not been extinguished but only confined. This power, though nebulous, remains ready for expression, and the teen is compelled to find some way to put the power back in force for real. He rebels against the authority of other people, especially parents, and enters a search to find a clear channel of expression. Besides the constraints of authority, another enemy of his power is lack of self.

The teen, driven by social pressure, must decide on an identity, true or false, that will lead to acceptance by the peer group. He has forgotten who he is, for the original self of early childhood has internalized so much information, accurate and inaccurate, that the self barely whispers. The adolescent must pick and choose to find an identity to "try on for size." These years are, then, a period of experimental power and experimental becoming.

The adopted self of adulthood is a combination of the earlier expressed opinions of others plus the experimental choosing of a personality in late adolescence. The sense of becoming has been compromised by this conglomeration of mostly inaccurate information. If the experimental personality has become a comfortable fit, the illusion of power will return. If the fit is uncomfortable, unworkable, or in stark contrast to the true self, an illusion of powerlessness will result.

Power and Self-Esteem

An illusion of power will result in a seeming self-confidence, while the illusion of powerlessness will give birth to a feeling of helplessness. An adult with seemingly high self-esteem and an adult with seemingly low self-esteem are equally deluded, since neither sense is based on truth.

High self-esteemers tend to accomplish more in life by the world's standards; but in times of crisis, they are just as vulnerable to psychopathology as are low self-esteemers. In the stock market crash of 1929, it was the successful that leapt out of windows to their deaths. Underachievers were in a much safer place, with much less to lose materially.

The roots of ambition are to stave off the fear of annihilation of self. The continual attainment of material things forms walls of false security around this fear. One worn-out man who came to me complained, "Everybody thinks I've got it made when they see my big house with two beautiful cars in the driveway. But they don't know what I have to go through to keep them."

I saw the man several years later and learned that instead of working on the discovery of his true self—the only way to real security—he had spent his efforts in a new business and had become a millionaire. He boasted, "I'm in multilevel marketing." When and if the pyramid scheme collapses, he will have a long fall, which could destroy him.

Many people are too busy getting further lost to ask directions. They go in circles, but they move quickly. Some rush toward the goal their parents have set; some continue a family tradition by taking over their father's business; others stalk a career they think they may enjoy or chase fantasies; and some do practically nothing. Some are financially successful and yet miserable and some are just miserable without all the pretense. Many are convinced they don't deserve any better than what they have.

Why Celebrities Become Drug Addicts

Earlier this year, our beloved Whitney Houston, a national and world treasure and precious person, has recently died. The medical examiners have not yet reported fully, but there is evidence that various prescription drugs were found in her hotel room.

If the evidence indicates that she died from an accidental overdose, I would not be surprised, the reason being that she was a major celebrity. I would also not be surprised if further investigation into her childhood reveals that she was somehow either abused or neglected. But most likely, there is some major factor that led to an incomplete development of personhood. This is the reason that music and movie stars are prone to addiction. They do not have a strong sense of who they are in reality.

They lose themselves to their identity as performers. When one does not have a firm hold on his or her true self, there is "no-one home" to deal with the enormous stress of stardom. The character she presented to her public was very convincing, but chances are that she was not convinced—not certain that she was really the person that the public loved so dearly. Her close friends did in fact know the real Whitney as a very kind, caring, and generous soul. She gave of herself all of the time according to those who knew her best. But as with many of our most famous heroes, she may have given her "self" too much.

Young People Become Their Peers

Young people set the course of their lives not by seeking their true identity but by imitating their peers, adopting TV advertising propaganda at a deep, permanent level, and taking to themselves the ethics promoted on radio and in the movies. They purchase icons in the form of clothing labels, and take their contempt for parents to the classroom, where they are encouraged in more defiance by their classmates. They placate themselves with the illusion of power, with the belief that they already know all that is worth knowing, so that there is nothing more to be learned.

Both teens and adults miss the minimal educational requirements for a fulfilling, meaningful life when they fail to discover who they are. An ecstatic preacher, at the pinnacle of his sermon, shouted to the faithful, "You are the Pearl of Great Price." But these words only deepen the sorrow of a person without a sense of being. They feel they are the exception. Perhaps every other person on Earth fits in with this wonderful claim, but not them. What, then, can be done for the man who seems to hate himself, or for the woman whose mind can't be changed that she's not worthy to live?

A partial answer for many forms of psychopathology is to look back and dissect the false information conveyed early in life and then to rediscover self through exploring hidden talents and abilities. The self has been covered up but not destroyed. The self cannot be destroyed but only concealed.

A beginning is to work on recalling who we were at the earliest times, before the product was tampered with, and by seriously trying out all the character traits, wishes, dreams, and fantasies of our child. This process, under the guidance of an insight-oriented therapist, is a start toward wholeness. This attainment, in most cases, is possible, regardless of age, because the child within us is unchangeable. Many believe this child is eternal.

3

Lies Implanted by Abuse

Of all the horrid ramifications of child abuse and neglect, the self-beliefs formed by the child reap the greatest destruction. Abuse is the most penetrating and permanent communication possible, and it always conveys to the child one or more of several messages:

- "I caused it to happen." (Power or the illusion of power, depending upon the developmental stage)
- "It's my fault because I am bad." (False information internalized, encapsulated)
- "I don't deserve any better." (Erroneous judgment about self)

Sexual Abuse

The most frequent type of maltreating female children by far is sexual abuse. Whether the victim is very young or a teenager, she takes deep within herself all three messages above and develops a loathing that is all-consuming. Set up by either the taste or illusion of power, the girl concludes that there is indeed something horrible and detestable within her that caused the older person to perform such an act upon her. She knows little else but this: She is the one to blame.

Taking on the blame, however, does not explain the incident. The event makes no sense. Therefore, as a computer cannot process illogical inputs, the human mind, whether child or adult, cannot deal with events that make no sense. There is no resolution because there is no logic.

Since intelligent people tend to force sense into an occurrence so that it can be processed, the child tries to solve the mystery experimentally. A child molested early in life will be repeatedly drawn to the subject of sex, so much so that a seductive quality will seem to exude from the person until, if ever, the puzzle is put together. In addition, the victim will reflect a woundedness that is easily spotted by a predator. This is certainly one pattern. If I see a pre-teen with sexualized behavior, I know I am looking at a sexual abuse victim. However, there are other typical reactions. One is the overweight girl who dresses dowdy. Another is the Amazon warrior out to fight the world.

Because child molesters, as well as rapists, are predators, they have a capacity beyond the usual to recognize easy prey. Just as a hawk will circle above until it finds a wounded animal and then suddenly sweep in for the kill, a human predator acts in much the same way. This almost paranormal ability of human predators, combined with the woundedness of the victim, explains why, in so many cases, a child once molested will be molested again; and a woman once raped, will be raped again. I don't think this field of human activity is any different from some others. The same is true for school/workplace bullying and for violent crimes such as robberies. It can all be quite adequately explained by nonverbal signals sent out by the victim-to-be. A school bully will prod at everyone. Those who respond with emotion of any kind (fear, tears, aggression) provide amusement, and so will be attacked. Those who shrug it off are left alone. The same is true regarding sex.

Laura's Story

A Ph.D. candidate in Christian psychology at our seminary has volunteered to include her story in her own words in this book with the prayer of helping others find comfort and hope. She very successfully made the journey from patient to professional. She is happily married and the mother of three sons. (We have obscured her name for purposes of maintaining confidentiality).

This account represents probably the most extreme example of child sexual abuse that you will ever encounter. Her recovery has been so complete that she wrote, "Father, I would want you to use my real name; there is no shame in what we go through." As stated, the following pages are Laura's own words:

~ ~ ~

I wanted very much to write about my experiences and my healing from extremely painful experiences and how my faith contributed to the healing process. I have thought a lot about this topic, wondering what experience/s would be best to talk about. Truthfully, not to be dramatic, but my whole childhood was an agonizing experience. So it's hard for me to hear the words when someone says, "Remember the good too."

If any of you are or have been in recovery, and attended child abuse recovery groups of some kind, they often will say, find the good times to think about too. For me, the "good times" were honestly far and few between. As a child, I did do what I could to be happy, as all children do. We are innocent; we numb out; we develop coping skills that help us survive, knowing nothing else compared to our experience. In fact, what we go through seems normal to us because what do we have to compare to? Children are resilient (resilient in childhood to survive, but the repressed pain always comes out later, often baffling those who experience it), always trying to find the best in an abusive situation. This is especially destructive to the soul when you strive to find the best, a wonderful human quality, but have no other choice except to bond to the "bad" and to have to call it "good".

My childhood was full of chaos, emotional abuse, physical abuse, and sexual abuse. Let me share some background information:

I was born to a white middle class family in Riverside, California, in 1968. My parents appeared to be normal, if you were to look at them. My father was a school teacher and my mother was the "perfect" homemaker. Her hair was always perfect (up in what looked like an ocean wave), her makeup straight up Mary Kay, and the house always immaculate. Our neighborhood was one mile from the freeway, a mall, and nestled among orange groves with a horse ranch nearby. The tract housing lined up with only a few variations in the models of the homes and the colors. Each one was neatly presented by its owner attempting to show their uniqueness, their individuality.

Each house had a nice lawn, with one or two or more trees in the yard, offering a cool place to sit in the Riverside heat of the summer. But not my house. The yard for my house was covered in rocks, and cactus beautifully arranged from pebble rocks to walk on to large rocks you could sit on. And the cactus ranged from aloe vera to the tall pokier kind and the small barrel ones, with different kinds in between, all offering a painful poke to a curious child.

The difference of our yard perhaps indicated how different my family was. I don't know what happened in other people's houses, but I do know that my house was as cold as the big rocks I sometimes sat on between the cacti in my yard. The backyard was lined with poisonous Oleander bushes, that came with a warning from my mother not to eat them; but in my curiosity, I did taste the juice of the bush, and although I didn't die, I do still have a memory of the awful, gagging, bitter taste of that plant. This warning from my mother is one example of what seemed like numerous setups by my mother to me.

She seemed to be saying over and over to me in my life that, here is this poison or abusive person or drug, Laura; don't do it or use it or go there; but then turning her back, she would either leave me alone and/or leave me starving for attention so I would be a prime catch for a perpetrator. She left me alone to get hurt. So my front and back yards did not seem very child-friendly and neither were my parents, even though my father was a high school teacher and my mother taught piano lessons; they didn't have any outward obvious flaws; no snarling, or drooling, or tattoos, or whatever. They looked totally middle class, white, 1950s-style. But their inward flaws could not be hidden from us kids.

We did have a lawn in the backyard at one time, but my mother let it die probably around the time of my parents' divorce. So all that was left was dirt and some trees, each of us children claiming one of them to be their own. That was one thing I felt was my mine, my fruitless plum tree. I climbed up in it often and then onto the roof, just one of my special hiding places.

I was the youngest of three children. Interestingly, I was the only blood child of my parents. My mother, who was born in 1927, had an illegal abortion when she was a teen, and it left a hole in her uterus that she didn't know about until I was born. She always had miscarriages after that, never being able to carry a baby to term, until me. But my parents wanted children long before I came, and so they adopted my older brother and sister.

Because my parents never found truth in their lives and lived with mental illness and addiction (sex addiction, RX addiction), they were not good parents. There seem to be numerous reasons why parents abuse their children, and often the pain a child experiences is because of ignorant parents, parents who are hurting and don't even know how to meet their own needs, and I believe that these were some of the reasons for my parents' treatment of me. But some of what they did also seemed calculating.

My father was adopted himself in 1924 and must have felt that he was different (in a bad way) because he always pointed out the difference of admittance into our family between my siblings and myself. They were adopted and I wasn't; so when I asked for a hug, like an assertive and pained and needy little girl might, my father would tell me, "No, I don't want your brother or sister to think that I prefer you." I remember thinking to myself, "That doesn't make any sense; just hug them too!" But the reasons that adults behave the way they do are complex and when they behave abusively, it is attached to some kind of false belief, and I can only guess why my father was cold and angry to me.

Did he resent me because I was from my mother? Did he want to punish her through me? Did he really believe showing me affection would hurt my siblings? Or was he just unable or disinterested in giving me proper affection and this was his excuse not to do it? I don't know. But the effect was my being hysterical, begging for hugs, him prudishly looking at me and refusing to touch me with an indifferent look on his face. This was after my parents divorced when I was five.

Before that, my memories are sketchy; so I won't go there. But I do remember praying a lot as a little child, and I do remember my parents having a lot of anger that scared me—cussing at other drivers, yelling at us kids, and other things. My reaction was to pray, a sort of compulsive prayer, over and over. I was already showing great signs of anxiety and dysfunction, but I knew what source to look to.

The next memory I recall was looking at my mother in bed; she had tried to kill herself. She lived, and from that point on, my parents took whatever opportunity they had to make the other parent look like, well I can't use the words they used, but many cuss words were involved, and vulgarities.

My mother joined a singles group and started having parties at our house. A single mother is a child molester's dream, and that's just what happened. My mother, out of her own desperation for love and her inability to protect or care for her children's emotional well-being, hooked up with a child molester, Lenny.

He would take us all to nudist camps, ignoring our protests to get naked in front of each other and in front of strangers. I'm sorry for the rough content that I am going to tell you now but it's important to know what happens to people and it's important to be able to tell the truth of what occurred, and for many to hear the truth, if any positive change can ever happen.

Sometimes he and my mother would have sex in front of us, invite us to watch them, and have my brother take pictures of them in the act. They had sex on our kitchen table, with all of us standing around, them explaining the details of what was occurring, as if we were in a biology class or something. Lenny also would have me bathe him, focusing on "special" areas. He beat my brother in front of me, screaming at him (punishing him for having a healthy angry reaction to the disgusting abuse), and then picking him up by his ankles and dipping his head in the toilet. I remember that scene very well, I could buckle to my knees now thinking of it, wanting to help him, fearing for my own life.

My brother terrified, I tried to comfort him; but in his shame and anger, he lashed out at me and ran away from me, leaving me alone in the situation. Then Lenny told me to bathe him and molested me. This sort of behavior, including teaching me to use "self massagers" after some kind of education session, went on for about a year. Lenny justified molesting my sister and me by saying, "We don't want them to be frigid adults."

At the same time, another child molester was coming by to "visit" me and would molest me. Jack would take us all to get ice cream, fix my mother's appliances and when he was able to, get me alone and violate me.

My mother didn't spend much time at home at this time and me being 5-6 years old, I was totally unequipped to care for myself on any level. And when my mother was home, she was a very mean person. She would yell at us kids most of the time, wake us up in the middle of the night to do chores, often with a toothbrush to scrub the floor, our own toothbrushes because then, "maybe us damn kids might learn to be clean."

She was an emotional wreck, most likely bi-polar or something! She would be up all night, playing the piano and crying and come and get us and lecture us, spank us, sometimes focusing on my brother's private parts, repeatedly spanking him there. My brother became a very angry, hurt young man, as you could imagine.

My father didn't make up for any of it, as my brother reported years later that my father molested him. One time when I confronted my father as part of my healing process, I shared what I thought he didn't know. His response, seeming so out of the blue, was, "Children don't remember anything before the age of 3." I never said anything to him about anything before 5, so I don't know why he said that. He also said after I told him of some of the sexual abuse, "Well you have had quite an extensive sex life."

There was no hope for any comfort from him but only his hammering home his true belief that I am bad, I am flawed, I should have been more cooperative to the abusers, and that he only sees me as an object too, not as a person. So you know the adage, "crap rolls down hill;" well, my brother took his anger out on me, my sister did too, and their prematurely stimulated sexuality as well. My brother was a leader of the neighborhood recruiting other boys to help him chase me down, tear off my pants ("pants" me) and force my legs open, pin my arms down to look, touch, and insert objects. This happened so many times I couldn't count.

But my terror and screaming and crying didn't stop it; my mother didn't stop it; and these attacks seemed to trigger separate attacks from the boys in the neighborhood, sometimes chasing me down on my bike and dragging me off of it and into their bedroom, or coming in my backyard and assaulting me there. They all must have seen me as an object to do with what they want, gaining courage and permission from the previous attacks.

So from age 5 to 9, my brother beat me often, and my sister was abusive to me as well. They both seemed continually annoyed by me, by my fears; by me, period. Being significantly younger, they could demean me and shove me or punch me, and I pretty much could do nothing about it. My sister took after my mother in so many ways; both of them seeming to take joy in seeing me suffer. And the sexual assaults were almost daily, if not daily.

Instead of us children bonding together to help each other through the abuse, my siblings turned on me and each other; and because I was the weakest and youngest, I guess I was the target—oh, and I wasn't adopted, so maybe that gave them more hate for me, thanks to my dad for making that an issue. My mother also added to the confusion in other ways.

At age 9, my step-dad came into our lives and he is my personal Angel. At 9, the sexual assaults subsided from my brother, mostly because we finally got a real parent in the picture, if only for a few years. He stopped a lot of the abuse, but the anger and hitting did not completely stop, especially when he was away, out on a ship, as he was a merchant marine.

I cried a lot as a child, and I would often cry at night, many times calling for my mother; and yet my mother never comforted me. I would often not go to the bathroom because I would be alone in the evenings a lot and so scared to go to the bathroom, that in the middle of the night, when my mother was home, I would cry out for her to help me to go to the bathroom; she would ultimately come to me but it would take a while for her to come into my room. Honestly, I don't know if she enjoyed hearing me cry. But when Raymond McKnight, my step-dad, was around, he would come into my room, pick me up, carry me to the bed he shared with my mother, put me next to her, and go and sleep on the couch.

She never comforted me then either, but I remember Raymond's love.

When I was about age 11, my sister met a couple, Drew and Judy, on a train, when she was on a vacation she took when she turned 16, back east to visit our grandmother. They started to talk and found out they had something in common—nudist camps.

My mother's "ex", Lenny, was long gone and we had stopped going to nudist camps, but somehow I ended up going again. My mother never met this couple until the day they came by to get me. She allowed me to go with them, against my will, to the nudist camp. Just me, 11 years old, and this couple! I remember pacing the kitchen floor watching these new people and my mom talking with them about me going with them to the local nudist camp.

I did not want to go, but I thought they were cool when they let me smoke. I was already smoking cigarettes by then, but not in front of adults. I started smoking regularly at eight and drinking alcohol, then marijuana at age 10.

Drew and Judy were child molesters, and over the course of about two years, they abused me, brainwashing me with lines like, "if you had a real father, one who loved you, you would want to have sex with him," and "your mother is crazy," etc. Their perversions included taking pictures, all of this with my parents' implied approval (I can't say what my parents did know for sure. All I know is that they never talked with me about it and I was forced into the relationship even though I initially resisted.) One day, they, Drew and Judy, said I and some other girls would go to a photographer for modeling. They had quite a long list of girls that they offended.

Now, remember I am still just a little tomboy girl who is high half the time and anxious and tearful much of the time. I was always faking sick so not to go to school because I just couldn't deal with being there. I was a scared mess, partly from my siblings' teasing me, partly from being left alone so much, partly from already enduring numerous sexual assaults and physical assaults. When my siblings would leave me alone in the evenings, they would reinforce my fear that monsters would come get me and/or bad guys. And there was truth in their statements. The more frightened I was, the funnier it was to them. How is that sexually attractive to anyone?

I was grateful not to be left alone, and I did appreciate getting to play Atari and smoke and being told that I was likeable in ways from Drew and Judy. I was young and clueless and I didn't pay attention to much around me, not able to comprehend as an adult would, and so I never knew where I was being taken when I was in a car. Being with Drew and Judy was better than being home, isolated.

On the day that Drew and Judy took me and a few others girls to the photographer, I felt this prompting, almost a voice, but a clear command, "Memorize how to get there." At first I sort of ignored it, but I felt it, heard it again. I listened. I was in the back of their pickup truck and looked out the shell window, memorizing those Santa Ana streets, 14th, 7th; the building was brick, not red brick, but ugly tannish bricks. I obeyed the "voice" and memorized the way there. I was compelled to do so; I even remember thinking, *but I never know where I am at!*

That day the photographer only took headshots of us, and that was it. I remember walking in the studio and seeing a Rubik's Cube on his desk and asking him if I could play with it. I was met with a cold glare that caused me to look away and sit down politely and fearfully. I thought to myself that he wasn't very good with kids.

The next day Drew was on the phone with him, offering me and another girl to pose for nude pictures, and although that was going on as regular activity at their house, this seemed more sinister and I said to Drew, "No I won't!" He just glared at me and told me to shut up. He usually was coercive but not so forceful. He was changing, losing patience.

That week they were busted (thanks to the photo place turning them in), and I was now involved in the court system. I had detectives, was put in a shelter home for a while, and when the Orange County detective asked me if I knew where this photographer was, I said, "yes", remembering my memorizing of the way there. He said that Drew and Judy told him that they didn't know the photographer.

I said they took me there recently, and then I took the detective there. I don't know what came of that, but what I do know is the Spirit, God, told me how to get there. And the photographer must have gotten busted and was prevented from hurting other children; that is my great hope anyway.

The detective told me that the photographer had actually murdered children on camera, made snuff films. I was spared. *Why!?* I don't fully understand why, but to be honest, I resented many times being spared when I was in such agonizing pain during the healing process.

I have often felt that I shouldn't have been spared, but that is my sense of self-worth that at times is just about nonexistent. But I know for sure that I was "told" to remember how to get there and that there was a reason; I never have questioned that. I have only wished for more opportunities to be told where these types of criminals are hiding.

After Drew and Judy, there were other molesters, other abuse, and drugs. After the Drew and Judy episode and court experiences and being put in a shelter home and then foster home, I got home from the shelter at age 13. Having gained no healing, still seeking escape with drugs and alcohol, I was more vulnerable than ever.

One who had introduced himself to me initially as a friend, Guy, a much older friend, ended up requiring violating me to keep that friendship and flow of drugs. He was a neighbor; again pictures were taken; and I believed he loved me. But what he really did do was hook me on methamphetamine. He also got busted years later, another court case I was involved with. Again I was not the only victim. But I felt deep within my being that I was bad; I was stupid; I was shameful.

I was raped at other times, by "friends" that I had no clue how to protect myself from. I was unsupervised; I had imprinted in my soul that I was good for one thing only, and no one seemed to care unless they were looking to violate a young girl. I was coerced and manipulated, and almost always, I immediately made it okay in my mind by pretending he was my boyfriend or by getting high. I did resist, but just like when I was little, my resistance was met with more force. There were more than a few perpetrators, opportunists; some violating me once, some more than once. I just seemed to find them, or they me. The drug crowd isn't safe, but then again some teachers are not safe either, or parents who look like average middle-class white professionals.

Again with the resiliency of a child (temporary resiliency), I somehow found the strength to keep going, to find something to live for, if only for a bag of weed. I did have dreams, but I started to buy into some of the indoctrination that I was being fed to justify violating others. I didn't ever want to hurt anyone else, but I had no clue what that meant, let alone what it meant to protect myself at all.

Until age 17, my world of drugs and sex intensified. Then a miracle happened. I found a way out. I joined the Church of Jesus Christ of Latter Day Saints, the LDS church. Missionaries patiently taught me the gospel for almost a year, showing a form of love and patience that modeled God's love for me. I realized that it was okay to say no, to not want to, to expect more from people. I discovered that I am a child of God and that there are people who want to help and that I even had power to help myself, with God's guidance.

After I was married and in my early 20s and long past being victimized, I had embarked on the healing process. I married a man who was nothing like an abuser. My Heavenly Father set us up (I like to say) because if left to my own, I would have picked someone not healthy. But my husband is a patient and kind man, an abuse survivor himself; so he and I have taken this healing path together. Nonetheless, I was living with the debilitating and excruciating consequences of abuse; so was my husband, and ultimately our children.

The healing path is a necessary road to take, but the worst side-effect of it—hurting the ones you love by not being who you are meant to be. Instead they witness your extreme anger, depression, sorrow, and they suffer too.

I discovered something on my healing journey, something that broke my heart when I was able to access some police reports that were part of my case/cases. I was able to get what was left of them. There was my mother's testimony about me in the report saying this about her 12-year-old daughter, "Well she is known to be gone for days, drinking." She was trying to discredit me to the detective!

There was no compassion of a mother towards her daughter—none! This was the beginning of my coming out of denial of my mother's involvement. Of course any healthy adult would know that a girl in that situation is in serious trouble and is being abused, but in my mother's sick mind, she was using me in some kind of perverse way to get people to feel badly for her. That is what I believe part of what my mother is about.

Although I don't recall being gone for days, unless she meant to Drew and Judy's, which she set up and encouraged, I do recall getting really drunk once at my brother's friend's house and their sending me home. I then stumbled in the backyard, passing out in the dirt. I was alone, face down at 12 years old in the backyard, passed out drunk, and waking up the next day to my mother glaring at me with a hateful look through the window of our living room, watching me—not helping me, not worrying, just hating me. I got up slowly and stumbled in the house and was alone to care for myself after such an episode.

I don't know why my mother seemed to hate me and had no desire to protect me, but that's who she was.

My father was inappropriate too, mostly verbally, telling me about very disgusting sexual practices and giving me the overall impression that I was bad, not for being molested, but because I allowed the police to get involved and hurt the people who were having sex with me—as if what they did was okay, and I should be happy to provide sexual experiences for anyone who wanted them. It seems that sex is my father's religion that he preached and tried to convert often. Just like Drew and Judy, Lenny and Guy, plus many others, molesters always have a theory why it's okay for them to violate and even torture.

So how did I survive? God did not protect me from this abuse. I always believed in God, although there was a time when I was very rageful toward God. But I came to believe that He is there through all of our experiences, often weeping for us, whispering to our hearts that justice will come, that you will make it through this. It's just not in the plan that we will avoid pain. He does not cause the bad, but for Him to stop it would block our free agency and our chance to grow. I believe that we being eternal beings knew when we came to Earth that bad was possible, and we knew the range of badness. We just didn't know how it would feel. This life is just a tiny part of eternity, when we live in bliss, with no more suffering.

None of us is above another, and I am not better than the kids who lost their lives to the photographer. I am not superior to those who are still stuck in addiction, those who don't seem to be able to overcome in this life. We just all have differing purposes here on earth. For me, to make any sense of any of this, I must work to keep healing, to help others heal, try to find justice, to share a healing message.

I was literally saved. I got out of that old life by the grace of God. And I knew it then as I know it now that if I had not found the way out, the abuse would not have stopped.

There have been times I recall a prompting, a message, a whisper, here and there, saying to me as I cried and cried as a little girl, "You will not believe your future; you just don't know what you have coming to you. Don't worry; it will all work out. It's okay. I am here for you."

Although I was Buddhist from my stepfather's influence (and I loved my Buddhist experiences), I didn't understand the atonement of Christ. I believed in God and I believed it was all going to be worth it someday because He said so. The Spirit told me. I was able to maintain that optimism through all I've endured. At times though it did seem my optimism left, but temporarily.

So then at age 17, when I came across the LDS Church, I came to know Christ on a deep and personal level. It wasn't my plan to ever be who I am now, but it was God's plan, and I would rather listen to Him than to trust just myself. Even with the best intentions, if we don't have correct principles and true guidance, we will make a mess of our lives.

As I said, at 18, the abuse stopped. I was empowered by the new church's teachings, and I came to know the true nature of God and the support the church offered. I was rescued from the life I was in: drugs, sexual abuse, nothingness. I was literally saved. I got out of that old life by the grace of God. And I knew it then as I know it now that if I had not found the gospel, the abuse would not have stopped.

I would have had no way to support myself other than by being a sexual object, and I would have died from drugs or from an abuser if God had not intervened. And it was very clear to me that instead of that happening, I was now going to live a Christian life and somehow give back, if at all possible, what I was given.

You know, as a therapist, I get to work with people every day who have had trouble and pain of some kind and need help through it; I consider it an honor to be able to work with them. Although I don't preach or desire to preach, only to share truth, I do share true principles and this is the only way that I can hope to be of help. All truth comes from God.

All good and all truth come from God, so in that sense, I am able to share the gospel, the gospel meaning the good news from God; and if a client brings up God, I share with them, as the Spirit guides me (so I hope). With my education, my experience and my reliance on the Spirit, I believe I have become an effective instrument to help others in their healing path.

This may not sound like good news to you, but I know because I have been there that just because we love Christ, try to be like Him, live our lives as worthy as possible, we will not avoid pain. We will not escape abuse.

We will to some degree, as we can learn to protect ourselves in certain ways. But when I was a child, I was innocent, and these horrors happened to me anyway. I could not protect myself; yet God allowed it to happen; it was part of His plan that we agreed to; that is, not to have Him stop people's free agency, their ability to choose.

But although God does not always stop the bad, he provides a way for us to find our way out. So when I got baptized, it did wash away so much sin and pain, and it also opened the door to healing. And healing doesn't always feel good in the moment.

Ask Christ about it while He was on the cross, in agonizing pain, when He asked if this cup could be removed. Even He, the greatest of all, shuddered from the pain. We are in good company! He was the only perfect person and yet he was betrayed, spit on, beaten, killed. He descended below, all so He could know our pain, so He would know how to comfort us. And He knows that we will all be okay, in this life or in the next—that we will see the bigger picture someday; that we will know that it was worth it.

So how did I get through my childhood, and get the healing that I have so far? I prayed for the Spirit and I listened to the Spirit, always seeking the good, the healing way, and believing that God would provide a way. I was led to healers to help me, to good books, to personal impressions that helped me gain insight and correct the false beliefs I had about myself.

I have been weak at times and angry at God—not His fault, but it's something many of us do, get angry at God. And yet time and time again, He has been there, with the subtle whisperings of the Spirit, gently and patiently guiding me back to Him.

True healing has to be supernatural, from God. I honestly know no other way. If I did, I would share it. All good comes from God. And I know the only reason that I am able to function now and be even a small instrument in His hands is because of the healing that He has given me. I can now say that all of it has been worth it.

A couple of years ago, I might not have been able to say that, but I can say that now with complete confidence. It has all been worth it. I have the greatest gift anyone could have, and that is a strong testimony for our Savior; that even though I have suffered needlessly and by my own stubbornness, I know the way out. I know that He is there for me, and He is there for you.

Molested children are very often driven to sexual activity, seemingly on a voluntary basis, in order to find some meaning in the original event. For children, mysteries demand action to solve them.

The teen years, especially the early teens, soon after maturation, bring sexual acting-out behavior in order to figure out the meaning of the earlier victimization. She is not conscious of what is urging this sexual intensity as she violates her own values and morals for more experience; that is, more chances to solve the puzzle.

Before full adulthood, she will accept a significant relationship with a male who does not exceed what she unconsciously believes she deserves (message 3, above). Her partner will be physically and emotionally abusive, seeking to possess her instead of loving her. When she cannot stand the suffering anymore, or when there is intervention by a protective-services agency, she may be able to break the relationship, although the partner will continue to pursue her. But if she does break the tie, she will then go on to settle for another relationship that is worse than the first. Such is the case because the first confirmed what she "knew": that she deserved the treatment she received.

Because domestic violence shelters provide only protection and no effective therapy, their clientele nearly always return to the same man or find a more abusive one. The second relationship further confirms the original message, and therefore leads to still another arrangement with more severe punishment, and on and on.

Often the victim will have blocked the memory of the first assault, especially if she had been in a state of dissociation ("not there") at the time. In one case, two sisters, who slept in the same bed and were molested nightly by their father, were talking. The younger sister related, "It wasn't the dark I was afraid of. It was what would come out of it." The second sister replied, "What do you mean? Didn't you ever learn to go away?"

This phenomenon is the origin of Dissociative Identity Disorder (DID) and "multiple personalities", brought to public awareness through movies such as *The Three Faces of Eve* (1957) and *Sybil* (1976). In actuality, these false identities are not nearly as pronounced as popular belief would have it. There is a variance in speech, affect, and behavior; however, that is clearly noticeable.

This "going away" mentally is one form of dissociation and is a frequent "escape" from the intolerable and inexplicable. Dissociation and "repression" (the unconscious work of keeping a memory out of consciousness) are two of the reasons why child victims, and sometimes adolescent or adult victims, cannot recall the violation. However, the event does get expressed, as described above and as follows.

A 31-year-old mother found herself one morning standing in front of her dressing room mirror while holding a .38 revolver to her temple. Her finger was on the trigger, and it took every ounce of her will not to fire the gun. The urge had come seemingly from nowhere, without warning. She had never had such feelings before and had never been symptomatic of any psychological disorder. Had she told any of her many friends about the incident, they would not have believed her.

What was the cause of this strange happening? She had suddenly, for some reason, recalled the horror of being sexually abused as a young girl.

All during early treatment, she carried a blank look on her face; she was expressionless. She was emotionally numb.

Part of her knew her memory was correct, while another part doubted that such would even be conceivable. So she confirmed the truth by talking to a family member—an act that required admirable courage, perhaps even heroic. To my amazement, she required very little therapy after discovering the facts.

Her case, however, is very unusual. Because her sense of self was more intact than that of many people, she possessed an inner strength that enabled her to rapidly move past her trauma. Most victims require very gentle and slow-moving therapy in order to arrive at the place she achieved so quickly. Also, she had the advantage of being molested only once, while a high percentage of victims, as stated previously, are assaulted repeatedly by other offenders following the first wounding.

This woman was also spared having to go through "therapy" as a child. Many times, when a protective-services agency discovers such abuse, the agency multiplies the trauma by tearing apart the family and forcing the child into counseling by a minimally trained paraprofessional. The so-called therapy leads nowhere but continues for years.

Unless treatment is performed by a professional who is knowledgeable about the effects of abuse, the result is that the wound is driven deeper and made wider. Her condition is worsened by endless talking about, reliving, playing out, and otherwise keeping the violation fresh, alive, and full of energy. In addition, as with any therapy in which a child is the focus, the child takes on yet another false message: "There's something wrong with me." Therapy, therefore, must be gentle, focused, and limited by a time-frame with definite goals.

By means of therapy as brief as possible, the child must be brought to an understanding that she (or he) is not at fault and is not dirty or evil. The belief that "there is something deep and dark within me that caused it to happen" must be overcome by presenting the actual facts of the matter at a pace and in a manner that the child can tolerate. The child must come to accept that the blame lies with the perpetrator only, and that children do not have the power to manipulate adults to do horrible things. Treatment that goes beyond these types of understandings further victimizes the child. Any additional therapy should be at the choice of the victim, when she reaches maturity and can decide for herself whether further attention would be helpful.

An exception to the brief approach is family therapy, which is needed when the child is presented as the source of all the family's problems. The child can be relieved in this kind of bind only by treating the family members who would otherwise escape dealing with their own issues. Blaming a child for marriage problems or other family difficulties is a form of abuse in itself.

In my experience, a little girl molested by her father or step-father is often blamed by her mother, though not always consciously. The result, however, is that the girl is doomed to live out her developmental years in the midst of maternal hostility. Although it is usually veiled, the child can sense the mother's anger and jealousy. It can be imagined with little difficulty how emotional abandonment by the mother shakes the very foundations of the child's perceived worth.

Sexual Abuse of Boys

Not very far behind the prevalence of female child sexual abuse is the same type of assault upon boys. Hopper (1996) estimates that about one in six boys is molested before age 16. Through extensive interviews with male survivors, Lisak (1994) found that the impact of the event correlates with the increase in age difference between the victim and perpetrator—also, with the subjective emotional reaction of the child; that is, the child's perception of what was happening. He has obtained many dramatic self-reports substantiating the following themes:

- Anger
- Fear
- Homosexuality issues
- Helplessness
- Isolation and alienation
- Legitimacy
- Loss
- Masculinity issues
- Negative childhood peer relations
- Negative schemas about self
- Problems with sexuality

Other researchers (Briere et al, 1988; Fromuth, 1989; Hunter, 1991; Olson, 1990) have used standardized measurements confirming the following symptomatology:

- Anxiety
- Depression
- Dissociation
- Hostility and anger
- Impaired relationships
- Low self-esteem
- Sexual dysfunction
- Suicide attempts

Therapists working with men who were sexually abused in childhood have conducted clinical case studies (Lew, 1988; Myers, 1989) and consistently reported findings on long-term problems, including the following:

- Guilt and self-blame
- Low self-esteem

- Problems with intimacy
- Sexual problems, compulsions, and dysfunctions
- Substance abuse
- Depression
- Symptoms of post-traumatic stress disorder

Myers and other clinicians have observed confusion about sexual orientation; fear that the sexual abuse has caused or will cause homosexuality; and homophobia, an irrational fear or intolerance of homosexuality.

Every child, male or female, is vulnerable to sexual abuse, almost always committed by someone trusted by the child: parent, sibling, other relative, family friend, or caretaker (Grohol, 1996). This kind of offense includes more than the obvious touching or penetration and covers such perverse acts as exposing children to adult sexual activity or pornographic movies and photographs. Also included are having boys pose, undress, or perform in a sexual fashion on film or in person. Being spied on in the bathroom or bedroom is another offense. In short, sexual abuse is forcing or tricking a child into sexual awareness or activity for the personal pleasure of an adult or older child (Grohol, 1996).

Listed as some of the many forms of prolonged suffering that endures long after the event are (Grohol):

- Sleep disturbance
- Headaches
- School problems
- Withdrawal from family, friends, or usual activities
- Excessive bathing or poor hygiene
- Return to younger, more babyish behavior
- Running away
- Eating disorders
- Passive or overly pleasing behavior
- Self-destructive behavior
- Sexual activity at an early age
- Copying adult sexual behavior
- Persistent sexual play with other children, themselves, toys, or pets
- Displaying sexual knowledge, through language or behavior, that is beyond normal for the age
- Unexplained pain, swelling, or bleeding

- Urinary infections
- Sexually transmitted diseases

The Bottom Line of Any Type of Abuse

So far, I have discussed mainly sexual abuse, but abuse of any kind has dire consequences for the growing child. Let me interrupt in order to explain further to shed more light as my observations continue.

Whether the victim is male or female, and no matter what the constellation of resulting symptoms, the deepest ramification of any abuse, including neglect, is the disruption or derailing of the developmental process. The child is led down a blind alley when abused. If the assault takes place in the age range of 2 to 6, the child is blocked from exploring his true self; that is, his soul, with the result that he will not attain the critical grasp of his own personhood before that personhood gets further modified by outside influence. Therefore, future influence which might modify can mangle instead.

Tampering with the developing self in the period 6 to 13 robs the child of the illusion of power necessary for his personhood to survive the subordination period of that stage. Violations in early adolescence introduce a completely false personality at a time when the teen is already experimenting with trial identities; in other words, the adolescent is denied his own choosing of what will become part of the adopted self of adulthood. Thus, the adopted self will be farther from the truth than it would be if the child were able to experiment normally.

Whatever the developmental model, abuse of any kind, if severe enough, alters the personality at the deepest levels and shakes the foundations of self-development. If we look, for example, at Erikson's trust versus mistrust stage (Erikson, 1996), which is infancy, it is readily seen that even neglect, rather than direct assault, will result in the infant's learning that the world is a hostile place and that his own efforts to get his needs met produce no result. Neglect can be as damaging as the worst forms of active abuse. The same applies to the next age level, 2–6 years, with the further impact that shame and doubt will interfere with the struggle toward autonomy.

Abuse at any of Erikson's stages will disrupt the growth of self, both at that stage and on through succeeding stages, since a child cannot progress successfully until the conflicts of a particular stage are resolved (Freud, 1996). Thus, a child denied his basic needs in infancy cannot adequately explore autonomy later on. Guilt will override initiative at 4 – 5 years of age; inferiority will conquer industry at 6 – 11; and role confusion will cloud identity at 12 – 18 (Erikson).

The same principle holds true with my own model of the adopted self. The self of age 2 – 6 cannot be explored without the strength gained through the meeting of basic needs in infancy. The true self might then be nearly extinguished, instead of just subordinated later (6 – 13), and there may be little remnant of self in adolescence to direct the necessary experimentation of becoming. If the sense of power is denied in infancy, the child is robbed of the taste of power later (2–6), as well as the illusion of power (6–13), and experimental power in adolescence.

A developmentally disrupted child is doomed as an adult either to accept an adopted self that has little resemblance to the true self or, in extreme cases, to invent an imaginary self. The latter might explain at least one origin of psychosis. While mere symptoms—such as anxiety or depression—are caused by misinformation along the road of development, psychoses are the result of the wholesale denial of power and the nearly complete removal of any chance to discover one's self.

Secrecy

Children are abused in secret, for the most part, and are often issued dire warnings not to tell. Under-reporting by health-care providers is a continuing problem. Pediatricians, family practitioners, and other professionals sometimes wonder whether there is enough evidence to warrant the reporting of child abuse or neglect. Even though a mere suspicion justifies ethical action, facts are usually scant, and the professional is either repulsed by the idea of tearing a family apart needlessly or is in fear of a lawsuit. Again, very often children tell no one about their being exploited sexually, physically, or mentally.

When it comes to mental abuse, and sometimes physical, the child may not be aware that anything is abnormal about the way he is treated at home. Indeed, many highly abusive parents are proud of their parenting skills and see nothing wrong with their treatment of their kids. Same is true of many abusive teachers etc. The above factors plus the three messages described earlier make one wonder how prevalent abuse is in reality. The statistics cannot possibly be accurate but are certain to be far below the actual case. Obviously, a method is needed by which to help confirm suspected abuse.

The screening test beginning on p. 45 has been developed to overcome threats and other fierce intimidation that typically prevent a child from revealing the truth about past or present suffering. This is accomplished by basing the first half of items on symptoms rather than on reputed fact recalled from memory. The child is thus able, for the first half, to answer without fear.

The symptoms included have been derived from the general literature that deals with symptoms of abuse and emotional trauma. The assumption is made that since child abuse is traumatizing, symptoms of trauma will be present when abuse has in fact occurred.

For some reason yet unknown, when children take this test, they tend to begin talking freely during the second half, when the questions are plain and obvious to the child.

A second purpose of this instrument is to provide a means for interviewing the child directly, rather than through a third party or subjective psychological tests. This approach, because it is objective, tends to hold up in court proceedings, whereas subjective measures such as projective tests, drawings, or diagnoses made through play, call for an opinion of the expert witness. A subjective opinion by an expert witness, no matter how prominent, does not hold up well to cross-examination.

The inventory is designed primarily for use by child protective services agencies and forensic psychologists and psychiatrists, as well as by litigation support specialists working under an attorney. However, all of the following should be equipped with such a measurement:

- Attorneys
- Pastors
- Child protective agencies
- State Attorneys' offices
- Forensic mental-health professionals
- Domestic violence shelters
- Pediatricians
- Emergency departments
- Child psychologists
- Family practice physicians
- Psychiatric hospitals and hospital departments of psychiatry
- Community mental health centers
- City victim services agencies

Test for Concealed Child Abuse

1. I go hide so certain people won't find me.
2. I freeze in place and don't move for a while.
3. I roll up in a ball on the floor or in bed.
4. I lose the look on my face, and nobody can tell if I'm happy or sad.
5. I bang my head against the wall, on the back of my bed, on the floor, or on the back of the car seat.
6. Some adults have magic powers.
7. Some parents have magic powers.
8. My parents have magic powers.
9. Some adults can read your mind.
10. My parents can read my mind.
11. My parents have control over me even when they're not present.
12. My parents keep me away from other kids.
13. My parents never let me stay overnight anywhere.
14. I daydream or stare off into space, not really looking at anything.
15. I forget what I'm doing.
16. I don't feel pain when something should hurt.
17. I feel afraid but don't know why.
18. I feel guilty and ashamed, like I ought to be punished, even when I haven't done anything.
19. I get mad enough to break things.
20. I feel like a witch, or a vampire, or a snake, or a rat.
21. I try very hard to be perfect.
22. My parents are perfect.
23. I get real mad at some adults.
24. I get real mad at my parents.
25. I like to be close friends right away with grownups I've just met.
26. I have trouble sleeping.
27. I have trouble eating.
28. I sleep too much.

29. I eat too much.
30. I have aches and pains that people don't really understand.
31. I feel afraid, mad, sad, and guilty all at once.
32. I feel like hurting myself on purpose.
33. I have hurt myself on purpose.
34. I do things that are dangerous, where I will probably get hurt.
35. I am afraid to tell the truth about what somebody did to me.
36. I have been told by someone never to tell what happened.
37. Somebody touched my private parts, but I'll never say who it was.
38. Somebody hurt my private parts, but I'll never say who it was.
39. The person I won't tell on is an adult.
40. The person I won't tell on is an older child.
41. Certain people make me feel ashamed or bad or weird.
42. I share secrets with another person.
43. The person I share secrets with is an adult.
44. The person I share secrets with is an older child.
45. I am very afraid to tell the truth about what happened to me or about what I saw or heard.
46. I would get in terrible trouble if I told the truth.
47. Someone might be hurt or even killed if I tell the truth.
48. A pet would be killed if I tell the truth.
49. I want to tell the truth but I can't.
50. I would tell the truth if I could protect other people.
51. The people I would have to protect are:_____.

While this inventory has been greatly useful in my own practice, a comprehensive reliability and validity study has yet to be performed. Such a subject would be excellent for a master's or doctoral thesis.

Epidemic Proportions of Abuse

All of the following facts are directly from the U.S. Department of Health and Human Services (1996, 1997) and a Gallup Poll Report (1995):

- Investigations by child protective service (CPS) agencies in 49 states determined that just under 1 million children were victims of substantiated or indicated child abuse and neglect in 1997.

- In 1997, CPS agencies investigated an estimated 2 million reports alleging the maltreatment of almost 3 million children. More than half of all reports alleging maltreatment came from professionals, including educators, law enforcement and justice officials, medical and mental health professionals, social service professionals, and child-care providers. About 25 percent of these reports came from relatives of the child or from the child himself. Reports from professionals are more likely to be substantiated than reports from nonprofessional sources.

- More children suffer neglect than any other form of maltreatment. Investigations determined that about 56 percent of victims in 1997 suffered neglect, 25 percent physical abuse, 13 percent sexual abuse, 6 percent emotional maltreatment, 2 percent medical neglect, and 11 percent other forms of maltreatment. Some children suffer more than one type of maltreatment.

- Child abuse and neglect affect children of all ages. Among children confirmed as victims by CPS agencies in 1997, more than half were 7 years of age or younger, with about 26 percent younger than 4. About 27 percent of victims were children ages 8–12; another 23 percent were youth ages 13–18.

- Case-level data from 16 states suggest that the majority of victims of neglect and medical neglect were younger than 8, while the majority of victims of other types of maltreatment were age 8 or older.

- Both boys and girls experience child maltreatment. In 1997, about 52 percent of victims were female, and 48 percent were male.

- Many more children suffer abuse than are reflected in national statistics. Based on reports received and investigated by CPS agencies in 1997, about 13.9 children per 1,000 under 18 were found to be victims. In 1993, according to various community professionals, 42 children per 1,000 were harmed or endangered by abuse or neglect. A 1995 telephone survey of parents conducted by the Gallup Poll showed that as many as 49 children per 1,000 suffered physical abuse, and 19 per 1,000 were victims of sexual abuse.

Other authorities speak openly about alarm. In 1990, the U.S. Advisory Board of Child Abuse and Neglect declared the maltreatment of children to be a national emergency (Durfee, 1994). The board's chairperson, Deanne Durfee, proclaimed the tragic reality that each year hundreds of thousands of our nation's children are "starved and abandoned, severely burned and beaten, raped and sodomized, berated and belittled." They are also killed.

But most maltreatment is nonfatal. In 1992, fewer than 2,000 of the nearly 1 million abused children in the country were killed (Alexander, 1994). The numbers are nonetheless staggering. A subculture of "non-persons"—individuals stripped of their personhood—is gaining in population. Add to this the huge number, whose parents habitually use put-down statements, or use conditional love as a disciplining tool.

4 Physical Abuse

Head Injury

The leading cause of death among abused children is head injury. But again, most child abuse victims, in general, do not die. Most children, 70 percent, whose head injuries are correctly diagnosed and documented, have had previous head injuries (Smith, 1994). Wilbur Smith asserts,

> It is reasonable to assume, therefore, that some children's brain injuries are never detected and that there is a large degree of underdiagnosis, with an unknown number of children suffering subclinical abusive head injury, making published prevalence data artificially low.
>
> The mortality figures are merely the tip of the iceberg in measuring the pain inflicted by abuse. In most serious cases, the majority of children… suffer permanent neurological deficits. Even for those who survive without gross perceptible deficit, the outcome is not necessarily clear. Some of the "softer" signs of neurological injury, such as attention-deficit disorders, may result owing either to the injury or the chaotic environment that facilitated the abuse in the first place…
>
> Furthermore, we do not have any prior knowledge of the intellectual potential before injury… Did the injury knock 20 points off the I.Q. of a genius, rendering that child only high average?

These are usually very small children, from infancy through elementary school. Many cannot or will not talk. But what is the message about self when the person a child counts on the most in the trust-versus-mistrust stage strikes a blow to the head or throws the child across the room, down the stairs, or against the wall? The answer is that trusting is life-threatening. A message entering the mind so early in life has permanency due to its deep implantation. The child also concludes about the abuser: "He/she wants me dead." Even more devastating is the resultant belief that "If this adult wants me dead, then I don't deserve to live."

Exploration of the true self is halted as the false self begins to take over; both power and sense of becoming are suspended or removed. When a child is thus battered, he never wonders whether something might be wrong with the abuser. He always takes deep within himself the belief that there is something wrong with him.

A man in my care, Sam, now in his late 30s, lives under a bridge and eats from trash bins whenever he relapses in his struggle with alcohol. As a child, he was punched in the head routinely by his alcoholic father, for whom he holds no ill feelings. Since early adulthood, he has been billy-clubbed by police when resisting arrest as a vagrant. He holds no malice toward the police.

Periodically he detoxes and begins recovery at a halfway house that requires gradually increasing responsibilities as part of his program. When these duties reach a certain performance level, he becomes overwhelmed and confused, due to massive brain damage. He gets depressed and then full of both fear and rage. Then he drinks and returns to his "home" under the bridge.

A keen intelligence is evident early in his recovery efforts when he is neat, clean, and bright. Sam then shows a warm, friendly and cheerful spirit. When I look in his eyes, I know there is a person in there—a real one. But this man is totally unaware of who he is. His potential, probably very great before the brain damage, is untapped. Rather than clinging to an adopted self, as most people do, he has no sense of self. The early message that he does not deserve to live is blindly obeyed globally and is much too powerful and deep to be overcome for long.

Another man, Greg, in the same age group suffered regular childhood punishments of having his head slammed on the concrete floor by a crazed mother, after which he would be repeatedly taken to the hospital. Whatever brain damage did result, has not, surprisingly, completely stopped his intellectual development. The damage must have been localized by the head being stricken at the same site with every assault.

He has vivid memories of his mother parading around nude in front of him and his younger brother. He remembers being awakened in the mornings by his brother's moaning as Mother performed fellatio. He recalls sensing from early childhood through adolescence that his mother wanted him sexually, as well as his brother. As a teen, when he was dressed up to go out, the mother would comment, with a heavily seductive tone, "You look so nice."

One time in childhood when a new female acquaintance told him that he looked nice, Greg "flipped out" with rage and wanted to kill her. In this man's case, his most pervasive problem to date is rage against women, for every woman is a symbol of Mother.

His adopted self has two prominent features: "I am a sex machine humiliating women through conquering them sexually," and "I am an alien in this world without the authority to exist." His rage at times drives him near suicide, but the urge to self-destruct has been tempered through the realization that in his case, suicide would be substitute murder, the ultimate "gotcha." He has fantasies of pistol-whipping his mother.

The difference between Sam and Greg is striking. Although their abuse was similar, the effects are very different, as Greg uses his rage to survive and refuses to give up on life even though his adopted self tells him he doesn't belong on Earth. Their constitutions, being vastly different, add credence to the work of Gesell on individuality at each stage of development (Bechler and Hudson, 1986).

Greg has reached, and is succeeding in, the fourth developmental stage of Piaget (1932), in which intelligence is demonstrated through the logical use of symbols representing abstract concepts. The patient is an engineering student, now studying advanced calculus. Also, he is now aware, after some treatment, that women are symbols of Mother. Thus he now manipulates these people-symbols mostly in fantasies and not nearly as much in reality. In no way does this arrangement constitute a complete recovery, but it is an improvement over the actual humiliation of women driven by the compulsion to conquer on and on.

He did, until recently, have a long-term serious relationship with a woman who was "pathologically therapeutic" for him. Married previously for 11 years to an extremely abusive alcoholic, she had a continuing false need for punishment due first to some unknown early abuse and fortified by her marriage to the alcoholic. Thus she "triggered" her boyfriend by being jealous and seductive, just as his mother had been. He called her a "whore, bitch," and worse, by using the most destructive terms he could think up. Then he suffered crushing remorse and thus returned to her. She would forgive him, and then they would repeat the cycle.

The benefit to both was that the relationship provided a release. The unwritten agreement stipulated that neither would be physically hurt and that they would not abandon each other. They would continue to cooperate for each other's benefit. Thus the pathology of each was played out in a controlled setting under fairly clear rules. The "game" worked so well, however, that each continued to endure the extreme suffering, and they did not move on in their development as individuals. Many months of treating them both were required before they were able to separate.

In order to progress beyond this developmental-arrest period, they were required to disobey the messages of childhood. Children are taught above all else to obey. Rejecting the early programming constitutes betrayal and is thus unthinkable.

Shaken Baby Syndrome

The early clinical diagnosis of this abuse is usually obscured by a fallacious history reported by the parents or caregivers. In one study, over 95 percent of the initial histories supplied by the caretakers were false. According to Wilbur Smith (1994),

> We have received a correct initial history in very few cases, and even in those cases, the extent of trauma was minimized. The specious history often features a fall or choking event, rather than the true cause.
>
> The initial diagnosis is also confused because the child often presents in a state of extreme physical distress, near death. The life-support activities and immediate concerns of trying to revive the child and ensure survival take precedence over careful... documentation of bruising, and establishing the definite diagnosis." He warns doctors not to be misled by reports of short falls less than four feet.
>
> Serious injuries take serious trauma, and a child with serious head injury who is not involved in an automobile accident or a fall from several stories should be considered a possible victim of child abuse in the process of differential diagnosis.

Speaking of more recent studies, Dr. Ann Botash (2012) adds, "Intracranial manifestations of trauma are seen with inflicted head trauma or significant accidental injury, such as motor vehicle crashes, and may lead to significant morbidity or mortality in infants. In child abuse cases, these injuries often present with minimal or no external signs of trauma."

It is clear that an injury of this kind requires real violence—ruthless, hateful behavior against a child in the first developmental stages. At a time when he is testing the safety of his environment, he finds excruciating punishment without cause, totally unpredictable, unrelated to his own actions. He learns that crying for his needs to be met or crying because he is already in pain will lead to further pain.

Such a message, internalized at the earliest time, is implanted permanently: "I am helpless." "Nothing I try will work." "I will be punished for anything I try to do." "It is wrong and dangerous to get my needs met." Such communication will be the database to be struggled against as the child later seeks his personhood. The true self will be tightly constricted in its expression, and the base-line information will undergird each developmental stage thereafter.

The taste of power of toddlerhood, so necessary to propel later efforts, will be severely minimized if not obliterated. The illusion of power in the elementary-school years will be replaced with underlying fear of people and the global realm of the unknown. The experimental becoming of adolescence will be carried out, if at all, with great timidity. The adopted self, in the end, will be one of powerlessness.

Abdominal Injuries

This classification of child abuse is second only to head injuries in mortality. According to Dirk Huyer (1994), "High mortality rates in cases of inflicted thoraco-abdominal trauma may be explained in a variety of ways. Delay in medical treatment results from delay in presentation, inaccurate or misleading historical information provided by parents, and lack of information from the child. Because these features are frequently coupled with a lack of obvious external injury, a high index of suspicion is required."

It is not too harsh to conclude that there is little difference, if any, between a physical child abuser and a potential or actual murderer. These abusers are more than willing to risk the life of the child in order to conceal their venomous acts. They are murderous and full of deceit and self-protection. Most are repeat abusers and do, at some level, want the child dead at the time of the crime. In many cases, there are two abusers, each equally guilty, for one commits the assault and the other covers for the assailant. Parents presenting their child for treatment, if they do, confirm each other's story about what happened.

Huyer describes graphically the truth of the attack: "Direct blows crush organs against the immobile vertebral column or the lower rib cage with resultant laceration and hemorrhage. The hollow visceral organs (stomach and intestines) are filled with food, liquid, air, or stool. A direct blow compresses the contents, leading to sudden overdistension, with rupture spilling the contents into the abdominal cavity. With rapid deceleration of the body, internal partially mobile organs continue in motion with resultant tearing of intestinal mesentery."

The message to the developing child? "My body is a source of pain, not a source of pleasure." At a time when the infant or elementary-age child should be exploring and celebrating his body, he wishes he could get out of it. If he doesn't have actual physical problems on through adolescence and adulthood, he will be preoccupied with the subject. Pain in small amounts will bring fear, but he will not understand where the fear is coming from. He will not connect the present emotional distress with the earlier history of having pain inflicted on him, pain that does not go away in a few minutes but instead seems never to end. Thus, it is justifiable to ask whether such treatment is one cause of hypochondriasis.

Scourging

This category of corporal punishment includes the use of any instrument to inflict pain by whipping, whether by use of an actual whip, a switch, a belt, or another flexible weapon. Because this form of abuse is no less than torture and thus fully exposes sadism in extreme cases, and because tissue injury is visible, these victims are kept away from doctors. Otherwise, the secrecy is fairly easy to maintain, since usually the strokes are delivered to the buttocks and/or legs and are therefore out of view.

The first man I treated for post-traumatic stress disorder arising from child abuse was my most challenging case, due to his inability to control his yelling and screaming during therapy. I came close to being evicted from my office building.

While Lloyd was tortured all of his life, his recollection of events at about 12 are most vivid. His mother used to command him at will, always without provocation, to go outside and select a "good" switch. The rule was that he would be assaulted all the more if he did not select one that would cause great pain. It had to be long enough and green enough, strong enough, and flexible enough.

When he returned with the switch, he was made to remove all of his clothing, even his underwear, and stand before his mother totally naked and without moving. She would then whip him until she exhausted herself. She included all parts of the body, and made certain that she hit the genitals well. She stopped only when she was completely unable to deliver another blow.

Lloyd remembers time after time trying to stand still but slipping on his own blood upon the wooden floor. When he slipped, his mother became even more enraged. After each beating, all of them without notice, the boy crawled upstairs to treat his own wounds.

One time, while still bleeding from such a session, he ran out the door and all the way to the local police station to beg for rescue. He could get no help, because one of the officers was a sexual partner with the mother.

When this man first came to me at the age of 32, he was unable to speak during our sessions but only to scream, moan, and roar in rage. He was the most frightening patient I have ever treated. From late teens until a few years ago, he was repeatedly placed in one psychiatric hospital after another, in addition to jail.

He had become addicted to both drugs and alcohol, and remained an addict for years. Never in all of his psychiatric history was he correctly diagnosed but only assigned one false label after another, including socio-path, schizophrenic, manic depressive, and others. His true diagnosis from the beginning should have been "complex post-traumatic stress disorder", in my experience a condition very common to physical abuse.

After a long period of treatment, which began with daily, one-to-one sessions, and later progressed to male group therapy, this man has made a remarkable recovery. He is working full-time, living independently, and forming friendships. As a member of a very warm and supportive church, he has been working diligently on forgiving his mother. He traveled several hundred miles to see her when she was near death, and then went back again to attend her funeral.

My Own Personal Case

Now in my late 60s, I still have monthly or more frequent dreams of conquering my father, who has been deceased for nearly 40 years. I remember as a boy watching him proudly weave two leather dog leashes together for training the family pet, a pedigree Boxer. At the end of the two woven leashes, he attached a hard, wrapped ball, somewhat larger than a golf ball and nearly as hard, which he formed by tightly winding a long, leather thong. He left some remaining strips dangling loose off the end of the ball to resemble a cat-of-nine-tails. Even at my young age, seven, I wondered why a 250-pound man, a former amateur boxer, would need such a weapon to train a dog.

Not long after the project was complete, I was to learn that the weapon was not for the dog but for me. I had been accused of talking back to a teacher, something I had not done, as I tried repeatedly and frantically to explain to my parents. But my father took out that odd weapon.

I remember the horror of not being able to get away, incapable of standing, trying to scurry under the kitchen sink, only to be yanked straight in the air by one arm so my father could get another series of blows in. The first strike made me think I was being killed, but on and on it went, until I wanted to die with the next hit. I screamed as long as I could but eventually went limp.

Every time the "golf ball" struck, it pounded beyond the skin surface and wounded internal tissue, whether of the legs, chest, stomach, and almost everywhere except my face.

A few days later, when previously scheduled physical exams were conducted at school, the doctor asked what happened, upon seeing the black, blue, and yellow stripes with circular wounds from the chest down. I said I had fallen. The doctor did nothing. My life is described at length in later chapters.

The developmental impact in these last two cases? In Lloyd's case, the boy had learned that any action could bring punishment. From toddlerhood to about age 6, he was unable to learn right from wrong, because pain was random, lacking any cause and effect. Rather than having his chance at trial personalities during adolescence, he did not have enough sense of self even to begin the activity. There was no experimental becoming in adolescence, for there was no imaginary power to energize the effort. His adopted self became limited to an organism that felt nothing but rage and other deep pain. As a result, this patient's personhood needed to be constructed from the start during long, tedious, and wrenching therapy.

In my case, my developmental growth was too heavily dependent on my relationship with mother alone, for any remark or activity with my father was far too risky. The interaction that should have occurred, and the "Welcome to manhood" message that can be given only by a father never occurred. Thus, my male identity formation was delayed until my teens.

Fortunately, I became intimately involved with a female in my mid-teens, and the intense sexual relationship that ensured almost from the beginning more than confirmed my sexual orientation. I did, though, develop a seething hatred for teachers, since a teacher's false accusation led to my violent separation from my father. I became a substandard student, even though I was of very high intelligence according to I.Q. tests, and I had performed very well in school before my father's malignant sadism was exposed. Further, the educators who could have helped form my adopted self had less than no influence, and some of these teachers had been very gifted. A few of them really were lazy, though, and that infuriated me.

Lloyd and I were both plagued by the fact that a parent hated us. There is hardly a stronger block to self-worth than the belief that a parent hates you. Any child concludes that there must be something to hate and thus carries this conviction for life. When a child has limited or no value for himself (or herself), each succeeding stage of development is colored by some degree of self-hatred, with the result that the effort to progress is half-hearted and lacking in power.

Punching and Other Violence

After being almost killed with the dog device, I was warned that if that kind of punishment didn't work, then my father would "treat me like a man" and begin using his fists.

From the youngest age I can remember, I had always been taught to brutalize any other child for almost any reason, and so, being fairly large for my age through junior high school, had gained a reputation for being a fierce fighter (even though I suffered tremendous guilt after hurting another child).

At about age 13, I was accused at the dinner table of doing something I had not done, and my father thus had another delectable opportunity. He became insanely enraged when I began to beg him to believe me and persisted in not admitting any guilt. Father walked over to me, seated and just placing a fork in my mouth, he hit me in the left jaw with an uppercut so forceful that I was lifted up into the air and was sent flying into the corner of the room in a heap, momentarily unconscious.

I looked up and saw the blurred figure of my towering father standing above with clenched fists, a red face, and yelling, "Get up, so I can hit you again. Get up!" I was reduced to infancy and cried loud, uncontrollably, hysterically. At that moment, I felt destroyed, annihilated, melted down to deep shame over not being able to force myself to get up and take another punch.

I backed down from every other opportunity for a fight with other kids, even when confronted, for the rest of my teen years. One time, I let another teen snatch my bicycle and ride away. I gave up playing football in junior high and in fact developed a hatred for athletes. I quit the Explorer Scouts, quit trying in school, quit all previous interests, and resolved that I would do nothing from now on unless paid. So I got a job working as a dishwasher.

A few similar attacks occurred in my later teens. My father would get right up in my face and then "sucker punch" me, so that I would sail across the room and then hit a wall or the floor in a daze. I got to the point where I didn't care anymore whether he hit me or not because I no longer felt any pain from his punches. I had learned to "go away"; that is, dissociate.

Hitting my father, even though I had gained the courage by self-talk over the years, was unthinkable. I could not bring myself to hit my father. I felt that was the worst thing a son could ever do. But I did think of something that I could do that would partially restore my male identity: I could refuse to fall down when hit, no matter how hard. I mastered the skill of never going down, always staying on my feet after a sucker punch. From across the room, I came right back into my father's face and continue what I was saying, as though nothing had happened.

By about 18, I, as a young man, told my father that I was through paying attention to him at all and that I had no regard for him as a father, nor for his opinions. As a victim, I had made a tiny step toward becoming a man with this absolute rejection of my abuser. In a way, I had overcome my intimidator—not by force, but by denying my father's personhood as he had denied mine. I rejected my father's longstanding and repeated message that I was contemptible and had no right to become a man.

The dynamic of conquering one's abuser is one that plays in the mind of the victim forever. Because the abuser has robbed the victim of power, the power must be regained in some manner. Hence, the endless fantasies and dreams of overcoming the one who not only punished the body but raped the soul.

Back to the first man described—Lloyd. He had been subjected to a very broad range of sadistic abuse in addition to what has already been said. He was locked outside in the cold, beaten on the head with a bible as Mother quoted condemning scriptures, and forced to revive her each time she passed out from an asthmatic attack, usually caused by cursing at him until she'd lost her breath.

At about the age of 10, he was cooking dinner, as he did on those unforeseen days when there was food, and he happened to put too much spaghetti in the pot. His mother made him reach into the boiling water with his bare hand again and again until he had reduced the contents to the quantity she wanted.

It is no surprise that this man's recovery in adulthood required first doing something about the indescribable rage that he had carried all his life. Never did the child have a way to express this rage in his developmental years, for he dared not let his mother know. Even worse punishment would result if he let on.

Rage, being the strongest emotion there is, must find the exactly correct outlet in order to be disposed of. Rage is pain in the true self, as is anger. When present, rage dominates both the activities and the direction of every developmental stage. Just as no one can work while in severe physical pain, a child cannot conduct the "work" of development when crippled by pain in the soul. Rage of this kind, then, not only retards growth but can literally arrest development.

This man, therefore, was in many ways a child when he first came for help. He had no control over emotions, no inner strength to accomplish the normal duties of life, and very little knowledge of the world and its people. He needed to be parented for a long time, once the rage was dealt with.

Anger, the extreme form of which is rage, is unlike other emotions in that it must be directed at the person who caused it in order for it to discharge permanently.

It is obvious that physical pain is a benefit to the body in that it protects against further injury or a worsening of the cause. Pain is a warning signal that something must be done, that an injury has occurred, and that the body is in danger. So it is with the pain of anger: It is a warning that our soul is in danger or that it has already been injured, that something must be done to restore its previous health.

Anger, or rage, is a form of pain as necessary as physical pain. When we are insulted, humiliated, treated with contempt, or treated unfairly or outrageously, we feel the pain of anger just as unavoidably as we would feel physical pain in case of a bodily injury.

While anger can be *expressed* in any number of ways, it cannot be *discharged* unless directly aimed at the offender. This is the reason why the popular anger-management classes of today are not only ineffective but harmful. They result in the client's holding down and further suppressing the very pain that is so necessary. The pain is retained rather than used in a constructive way to care for the injured soul.

However, if the offended one goes to the person who caused the pain and simply states that the action or words hurt and that he will not tolerate such an injury again, the anger (or rage) leaves, never to return. Note that the client is not required to hurt the offender but only to object.

Even when the offender is deceased, this vital task must still be accomplished. The afflicted one need only talk to the deceased as though still alive, and believe that the offender does hear. Sometimes writing a letter to a dead abuser can be effective, and the same method can be used for others who for some reason cannot be reached. Even in cases where a victim dare not contact an assailant, as in criminal cases, a letter can be written but never mailed. The healing effect is much the same as a one-on-one interaction. Even more effective is voicing one's feelings into a tape recorder, without any censorship whatsoever; at a later time, it can be decided whether to send the recording.

Whatever the form of physical abuse, the results are similar, but the intensity varies according to the amount of physical pain and the amount of anger. In our society, children are beaten, whipped, punched, thrown, strangled, stabbed, molested, burned, pinched, and pummeled. To some degree, in every case, the child takes on false information and gets robbed of opportunity both in the developmental stage in which the atrocity occurs and in every subsequent stage as well.

<table>
<tr><td>**5**</td><td>**Terrorizing**</td></tr>
</table>

A Brother and Sister

While practicing in Philadelphia, I was presented with a brother and sister who could remember almost nothing before the age of 7. Both had suffered psychotic episodes beginning at age 15 and continuing through their 20s, with multiple hospitalizations. The sister was functioning to an extent, although heavily medicated, but she tended to get "sick" about every three to six months and required hospitalization again.

The brother was quite infantile in his thoughts and behavior and was extremely fearful and nervous all the time. Of the two, he seemed to be the most seriously damaged; yet he was the one most willing to stay in treatment, and he constantly worked very hard to move into new behaviors that were very challenging for him. Although he had been diagnosed as schizophrenic, I believed that his constellation of symptoms was trauma-induced. (The sister had been labeled "bi-polar" and thus had her "breakdowns" attributed to a chemical imbalance.)

I was unable to obtain any information from either parent in trying to find out the origins of their conditions, that is, what caused them to be this way. The mother did mention some small events in early childhood, but seemed unaware of anything major.

The father, living in a distant city, was contacted but categorically refused to offer any information of any kind. He said what would really help them is to stop all therapy and all medications. Being a long-term member of Alcoholics Anonymous, he suggested they join Al-Anon.

Both brother and sister held the conviction that they were terrorized as small children by their father, who was an active alcoholic during that time period. But neither could remember anything except being terrified of him then and in the present. They each had shadowy, vague, fragmentary glimpses of being used as experiments in the basement of their home. Their father had been a medical student in their early years, and they believed he used them for practice in a mock treatment room he had set up in the basement.

They both seemed certain that their father had a vile temper and used to scream at them and their mother. The brother thought that he himself might have been molested by a man whom he cannot recall, and the sister wondered if she might have awakened in her father's bed after having been drugged. Yet, all of these images were hazy, and neither spoke with certainty. It was as though they were guessing.

At one point during treatment, I commented that both the sister and the mother tended to over-react whenever the brother got upset and, further, that he was not encouraged in accepting responsibility. Without hesitation, the sister instantly responded, as though the words were coming out by themselves, "I think Mom and I are afraid my brother will let out a family secret."

In that family, there are secrets galore. These secrets are the terror that paralyzes the victims and keeps them that way. The secrets are protected by maintaining the position that the daughter has a chemical imbalance, that the son is schizophrenic. The cover-up in this family, and many others I have dealt with, would falsely lead one to believe that both brother and sister are "sick" from unexplained causes that are no one's fault and that nothing can be done except to medicate and periodically hospitalize.

Despite all of this denial, not all of which was conscious, it was evident that these patients were reliving childhood terror and that this crippling fear was maintained by the mystery of not knowing what had happened to them. Their fears and resultant powerlessness had become spooky and magical. Therefore, we began analyzing the only information we had: their delusions, hallucinations, nightmares and flashbacks, as well as their many fears.

These phenomena, though grossly disturbing to the patient, provide invaluable information. Just as analysts use dreams, full use can be made of hallucinations as well. *Every nightmare and every hallucination should be explored for symbolic or literal content*, for these representations, no matter how bizarre or seemingly nonsensical, originate in the reality of experience. The power of these frightening products of subconscious material subsides when the patient realizes that placing them in the light provides precious clues.

Through paradoxical intention, the patient moves from fearing these phenomena to regarding them as treasures that will help set him free. When this intention is applied, the true self is in control rather than the powerless adopted self, and the patient begins to experience the actuality of power while the eerie, mystical force of hallucinations and nightmares fades.

Even though we did not know the details of what had happened, we were able to piece together some conclusions that made sense to the patients and that could be processed. Neither has been hospitalized since treatment began about four years ago; their medications have been reduced; the brother has begun to seek employment; and the sister is more comfortable as a mother and wife.

Both patients are highly intelligent, and they have many abilities, but these resources will remain dormant until each discovers more truth about what was done to them. *Mystery is the great terrorist, and family secrets keep the dread fully alive.*

The most helpful accomplishment in this case is that these young people do not view themselves as hopelessly and mysteriously mentally ill. They now view themselves as victors instead of victims, who are yet reacting to the abnormality of someone else. There is power in their hope of discovering more about their past and thus continuing their process of becoming.

The Bedwetting Boy

In Jacksonville, Florida, I was presented with a 6-year-old boy who had undergone bladder surgery for a bedwetting problem. His mother, who had been in psychotherapy for 30 years, had been told by her most recent psychiatrist to consult a urologist regarding his son's problem. The mother had agreed, and thus the urologist recommended and performed bladder surgery. The surgery accomplished nothing, for the problem continued unchanged.

In talking with both the mother and the boy, I discovered almost immediately that the child had been living in the fear that his father would kill both Mother and himself. He had repeatedly witnessed the father, in a drunken rage, ransacking the house and threatening to kill them, and he had watched his father grab Mother by the hair and hurl her down a flight of stairs. The boy had been wetting the bed only after each of these episodes.

One 10-year-old boy was brought to me by his mother for a second opinion. Another doctor had recommended that the child receive weekly psychoanalytic therapy through age 21.

Clearly, the boy was upset, but his "disturbance" was the direct result of what he had witnessed. He had recently returned from a visit with his estranged father in a distant state. The father was living a completely unregulated homosexual lifestyle that included parading around nude along with his lover and performing all sorts of sexual acts in the presence of his son. (There is no implication here whatsoever that such behavior is typical of homosexuals.)

The boy's emotions had been ransacked by this horror. He had been so terrified by this first experience of seeing grown males fully erect that he had become grotesquely sick at his stomach and wanted to run, but was prevented. His emotions, heightened to the maximum, were conflicted among anger, helplessness, alienation, grief, and, of course, guilt. As every child does, he felt responsible for the debacle that had taken place.

The child's resultant needs were to understand that he was not the problem, that there was nothing wrong with him, and to be comforted as well as affirmed. Certainly no extensive therapy was required, and the child recovered very quickly. Had he not received this brief intervention, however, or had he been subjected to long-term "therapy", the impact of the trauma would have penetrated more deeply and would have become permanent.

Adolescent Cases

One mother of a 13-year-old girl was dismayed after divorcing the child's father and not being able to get her daughter to accept her new partner. The solution was to send her to boarding school. After struggling with this rejection for several weeks, the girl became noticeably depressed and was thus referred to the school's psychiatric advisor. Hospitalization was arranged immediately. Following two months of in-patient "treatment", the girl was sent home to Mother for a visit.

After the girl had been home a few days, the mother came upon a sudden realization: when her daughter was in boarding school, there were substantial costs; when she was in the hospital, the insurance company paid everything. So the mother went directly to the child and told her she wished she had never been born; that she was a hopeless case; that she never wanted to see her again. In perfect obedience, the child became very depressed and was re-admitted to the same hospital. When she began to improve under my care, she was reassigned to another doctor. She spent the greater part of her teen years, until age 18, in and out of hospitals.

Soon after I began my private practice in Philadelphia, a father brought his 15-year-old son to me. Having heard of me through a newspaper article, he was willing to travel the 150 miles to try to find out the truth about his son's condition. Before they had left to see me, the mother had called me and said, "They have my permission to see you, but I know it's not going to do any good. There's been something wrong with my son ever since he was born, and we've taken him to doctors all of his life. I've already told my husband that either he (the boy) goes, or I do."

An exhaustive interview with the father and son together convinced me that the absent one, Mother, was the one who needed treatment. For years, she had taken out her frustrations on her son and blamed him for all her problems, including the bad marriage that she herself ruled.

At the end of our one time together, I told the boy that he had been carrying a false label of "mentally ill" all of his life and that now he must remove it for good. I told him to discard the label completely and never to pick it up again. The father broke down and wept. Between sobs of relief and joy, he exclaimed, "I've always known at some level that my boy was all right, but I couldn't get anybody to agree with me."

In all of the above cases, it can be seen that these children had assimilated incorrect information about themselves. As every child does, they believed what was communicated about them, either in words or in deed, or both. By therapeutically removing the false "inputs" and reprogramming with facts, they were enabled to proceed with a more normal self-development so that the adopted self of adulthood would not be further removed from reality than for many people.

Notice also that professionals had done much to affix the label of mental illness in the first place. Victims get labeled while the perpetrators go untouched. The doctors had cooperated with the abuse of the parents by taking at face value the deviated histories presented by the adult caregivers. But just as parents render false reports in cases of physical abuse, they do the very same with mental abuse, especially with terrorizing. *When a doctor attaches a false label, it takes another doctor to remove it.*

Death of a Terrorist

One of the most emotionally confusing times in the life of an abuse victim is when the victimizer dies. The victim's reaction is bewildering. While the grieving process is absolutely necessary—for mourning should occur for any major loss, even loss of an abuser—grief is clouded and conflicted with other feelings, some of which have a "magical" quality for the patient.

In order to illustrate, I have included an excerpt below from an earlier work of mine (Castallo and Ewart, 1977) in which I describe for my character, a prominent physician, his own experience in seeing his abusive father lying on his deathbed:

~ ~ ~

Powerful fathers are not easily erased from daily consciousness. And to know that the most basic influence in your life is losing his presence brings on a recurring melancholy. Salvatore [father] had always been the looming object I needed to overcome—or at least equal—so that I could be a person myself. Through his long deterioration, as hardening of the arteries usurped his acuity, I felt an occasional pull of depression without fully understanding. Perhaps I was so unsettled by the way old age and circumstance had downed my father that I lost an adolescent goal to compete with him. I was ashamed of an immature motivation to overcome him and compelled at the same time to seek strength for myself.

There was nothing in the future that Salvatore could bank on. The old man had long ago issued his last command, and there had been nothing fearful in him for years. But even in his confusion, he moved with a remnant of dignity. Strangers could somehow detect that the big gentleman had been somebody.

Salvatore's doctor knew when to call the final visit—when to inform a close relative that death was forthcoming and that the family must gather soon or not at all. I was notified late one evening in February, only a few months after he had gone back to Providence.

As dusk approached on the following day, I was entering the house in Providence to see my father and to say goodbye.

He was alone and still in a room that looked unvisited, and I thought at first that he might have already passed. But as I studied his large frame from the open doorway, I was both relieved and frightened to see his big chest rise slowly and descend. I walked straight over to him and saw as I approached that he was wet and that the white sheets were clinging to his sweaty, tremulous limbs. He looked like a gigantic, abandoned puppet whose strings had rotted away.

His pure-white mustache stood out as the only spirited feature on a once-commanding face—that is, until his eyes opened. His eyes! They were clear, agile, and full of activity. They seemed to live on beyond Salvatore, seemed to be waiting behind in order to gather up a final image for eternal reflection.

I studied him and memorized every aspect of his presence that I could. Then, after only another moment or two, I grasped his limp hand, kissed him on the cheek, and promised to visit him in the morning. But I knew he would be gone.

Had he been different—or had I—or maybe if we hadn't been so similar—I don't know—then I might have loved him. But I did, and I do, fear him.

6	**Parentification**

A fairly common practice of parents is to make the child an intermediary when a fight is going on. When parents do avoid assigning the child this role, the child will often slip into the role without prompting. *Attempting the impossible and never giving up will always result in symptoms of some kind.*

Children forced to endure parental fighting or to witness one parent being abused by the other will suffer emotional turmoil, including fearfulness, becoming withdrawn (so that he does not have to take sides), or acting out as a behavior problem in order to draw attention to himself as a decoy and stop the threatening struggle. bedwetting, for example, or nonconformity in school, can sometimes accomplish a truce and also provide a way to vent the unavoidable rage the child feels as a result of what he is being put through.

If it isn't the marriage itself that is the source of the child's unrest, it is often another kind of unhappiness on the part of one or both parents. Every child who senses unhappiness, fear, or other distress in a parent will try to "fix" it. He will not only believe that he is able, but will actually take it upon himself as his own personal responsibility, often for life.

As already explained at length, children are not aware that their power is limited. In fact, they go through necessary stages of illusory, imagined, and experimental power (table 2-1, p. 13). Thus, children undertake the task of rescuing Mother or Father, or both. They try to be a better boy or girl, perform perfectly in school (or misbehave), be quieter or noisier when Mommy's upset, go to bed earlier, stay up late, stop fighting with siblings, start fights with siblings, try something different, or try everything harder. This is to achieve the goal of happy parents who are available to meet their needs. *When they fail, and they always do, it is their fault.*

In one case of this kind, I was a young woman's 30th doctor. Laura came to me at the age of 19, never having been out of the hospital for more than six months from the time she was 13. She arrived with the firm expectation that I would put her back in the hospital, as all 29 other doctors had done.

When the entire family was called into the office, everyone showed up except the father, who had long ago abandoned them all. The patient, however, deep in her subconscious, continued to hope that repeated hospitalizations would bring him back. Through all these years, the family had deteriorated through the mother's lost ability to govern. Laura believed that they were just as "sick" as she. I agreed.

They did not need to deal with this fact, however, because they kept their focus on the patient, who cooperated fully. She was the endpoint in every matter discussed, and the family was entrenched in a process of shunning their own problems by projecting them onto the patient.

All through the first family session, Laura was the only one openly upset. She spoke with emotion, cried, complained and argued; but the rest of the family stayed composed as uninvolved observers. When all of this was pointed out, that the patient was expressing all of the emotion for them, they seemed unconvinced. I suggested that the patient felt all alone in being the only one to admit the pain, that she was crying on behalf of them all, that she was suffering in their place. This arrangement was not fair, I contended, and it was too much for the patient.

Finally, one of the brothers sprang up and ran over to comfort her. Next, a sister followed; then, Mother. Before long, they were all weeping and yet with great relief because it was good to have everything out in the open.

All resistance and denial were given up by the family, and they began to talk honestly about the real causes of their suffering. The patient was relieved of her obligation to continue as "mentally sick". Instead, she began to lead her family into some deep insights about the way they had all dealt with emotional pain in the past. She never returned to the hospital.

Mixing children into parental struggles is pervasively, destructive simply because children believe what their parents tell them, no matter how preposterous. They try to adapt to the role they are assigned or place on themselves. *Children will participate in any and all madness.*

A child can have a role assignment even before birth, and sometimes before conception, as in the case of a child conceived as the final effort to save a marriage. Other parents, as mentioned, conceal the hidden agenda of possessing a child for life as an emotional support. Usually a daughter is chosen as a lifetime companion, but sometimes a son is so used.

Very often, we see a sad and feeble rebellion whereby a girl so singled out may resist to a point during young adulthood, even going so far as to marry, in defiance of her "duty" to serve Mother. Such unfortunates tend to marry someone who is sure to fail as a spouse, so that a return to Mother is guaranteed. This kind of abuse occurs more frequently in single-child families.

Debbie: 20-Year-Old Anorexic

A woman we'll call "Debbie" came to me at age 20 after several hospitalizations for anorexia. She had long ago been convinced that she did not deserve to live and in fact had no right to live. Mother had been addicted to alcohol and prescription drugs all of Debbie's life and had always refused any kind of treatment. She had chased the girl's father out when she was in second grade and from that time on made her daughter her "mother".

All during her elementary and high-school years, Debbie was a captive in charge of making Mother happy in a contract that guaranteed a no-win. The unwritten agreement was, "It's your job to make me happy, but nothing you do will ever work." While Debbie was still in elementary school, she had branded herself as unworthy to live because she was already failing at the job she thought she was born to do.

Mother had also taught her from the earliest age that she was not permitted to pray for herself but only for her mother: "If you pray for yourself, you are being selfish."

In her late teens, Debbie had made a kind of adjustment by becoming overly dependent on a tight network of very close friends who had taken responsibility for keeping her alive. In this mode, Debbie was allowed to be the child previously forbidden to exist. They sympathized with her condition and fussed over her until she finally ate, in obedience to her surrogate parents. At times, she took enough nourishment to stay alive for a little while, only to be overcome with the deep weight of failure, at which point she ceased all intake except water until she was again hospitalized.

One particular time, she had very nearly succeeded in starving herself to death, and the doctors did not know whether she would live or not. Mother came to visit her in the intensive care unit. With Debbie lying there near death, with tubes in her arms and hooked up to monitors, Mother exclaimed, "If you could just get over this, I could die in peace." Debbie did not miss the message: If she dared to recover, her mother would die.

One might reasonably wonder how such a victim could ever get free. For Debbie, the answer was the same as for everyone caught in any kind of bondage: the truth. She had to realize clearly in what ways she was acting in direct response to her mother; what her real responsibilities were; what roles were possible for her in life; and what part she had played in remaining a captive. She had to accept the fact that she must give up the impossible and begin doing the possible in every facet of her life. It was required, as terrifying as the process was, that she face the truth about what her mother had been doing to her all of her life.

Above all this, Debbie needed to discover who she was; that is, gain some clue as to her true self, a personhood having infinite value apart from any other person in the world. It had not been possible to come to a place where she could feel good about her "self" because her self had never been explored. She had to begin by discarding the false self that had gotten its power from misinformation and impossibilities; she had to drop the false self like an old coat, never to pick it up again, and start afresh in the light of facts.

A child may succeed in pleasing his parents, may make them laugh, may be a good student, may clean his room admirably, but he cannot make a parent happy or solve a parent's problems. Trying to make anyone happy, no matter what age in the developmental process, and no matter what the relationship, will create a "failure theme" with a strong component of pervasive guilt. Herein lies a major root of depression in adolescence and early adulthood.

Children of Alcoholics

The dynamic of parentification is both strong and frequent in alcoholic families. Many children of alcoholics who seek treatment in adulthood are unaware that their present distress is related to alcoholism in the family, no matter how far in the past. Most are convinced that there is inherently something wrong with them in that they cannot seem to cope, to live in peace with their intimates, or feel fulfilled in their life's work (if they have found it). In some regard, they tend to feel lost.

It must be remembered that an alcoholic in a family is a hurricane, so consistently powerful that the entire family is forced to adapt to the threat of imminent violence or a host of other forms of craziness. When a family "adapts" to craziness, they have formed a maladjustment that makes their situation seem normal. But there is no normal way for anyone to adapt to craziness.

Their ways of relating to each other, covering up the unpleasant, not talking about emotional subjects, learning to keep family secrets, all become a deep-set mode of functioning. The fallout of such entrenchment reaches down from one generation to another and to another.

As one example, it seems that the overwhelming majority of daughters of alcoholics tend to marry alcoholics, often more than one. As women tend to do, they are seeking to find their fathers in their husbands; but in their case, Father is a risky model in picking out a mate. Nonetheless, such a young woman will recognize certain personality traits that seem not only familiar but somehow enticing. Her own father, always inaccessible, seems available in another body. Seeing her father in such a one, she sees a chance to have her father at last, after all those years of being deprived.

There can be a conflicting need for such a daughter to gain her "father" but also at the same time to rebel against him. She can develop an unwieldy relationship in which both love and hate vie for the same space in her heart. In such a dilemma, she will seem to hold on too tightly and be prone to extreme jealousy and yet, at the same time, be subject to the sudden powerful urge to reject or punish her mate. She retains the deep and powerful need for her father along with an equally powerful need to vent her rage against him. Yet these emotions will be pushed aside when the alcoholic drinking pattern in her husband emerges—if the marriage lasts that long—and she will undertake again what has always eluded her: getting him to stop drinking. When she fails, it will be her fault.

The term "she" continues to be used here, for indeed it is most often a woman who comes for help when caught in this kind of a life-limiting problem. Certainly young men have been caused to suffer in similar ways, but they tend to handle their problems in a manner that usually remains outside the doctor's office. For example, when the husband is an adult child of an alcoholic and is playing out the consequences on his wife, whether knowingly or not, he will usually send his wife to the doctor. This is a trait of men in general, no matter what kind of problem prevails. Husbands, regardless of their role in the difficulties, all too often tell their wives, "You go. You're the one who thinks there's a problem."

A girl growing up in an alcoholic family will often be doomed to failure regardless of which parent is the drinker. She will be the peacemaker and the one who tries to protect one parent from the other. All during her developmental years, she hopes that if she tries harder, then Mom or Dad will change. Any child caught up in such a bind will eventually take on the self-appointed label of failure. Trying the impossible over a sustained period of time will produce this kind of condemnation in the adopted self, and she will likely spend a lifetime trying to overthrow the verdict. The theme will be played out on the eventual spouse and on the children, who will find that they also have a parent who cannot be made happy.

The failure identity very often leads such a child to over-achieve, first in school and later in most other kinds of challenges. They will have a tendency to become people pleasers, having failed so miserably with the most important people in their lives: their parents. They will also be prone to relationships of bondage with unreasonable, demanding, inconsistent people, sometimes tyrannical people, just like the ones at home during childhood. Sometimes they work out their early maladaption by setting the goal of becoming the ambitious, successful, family "savior", the one who finally brings some dignity to the family name. This course is the most frightening of all, because it consumes nearly all of one's energy. Failure is always right behind, no matter what the level of success, so to stop running would be unthinkable.

Because an adult child of an alcoholic has not learned what normal existence is, she (or he) must guess as she tries to make her way through life and possibly establish her own family. Whatever a child has experienced in her own family is normal for her, though by reasonable standards her "normal" might very well be crazy. A child brought up in confusion, plus the threat of imminent danger, or at the very least, constant insecurity, must seek by trial and error to discover what the real meaning of normal is. Missing what should have been learned in the family setting, plus having learned much in the way of irrationality, results in a huge learning void that must be made up for by direct, therapeutic teaching.

Such a young adult—or even a middle-aged one—will be further done in by nondirective counseling approaches that forever ask, "What do you think?" The patient is missing some vital information about what normal is, and it doesn't matter what she thinks as much as what she needs to learn. Thus, the therapist must be a patient teacher who is directive in his treatment.

These victims have difficulty following projects through to completion. They tend to shift priorities and feel that whatever they are working on at the time is the wrong thing. They have not been taught how to establish priorities because they have been raised in a home where there has always been but one priority: keeping the peace and avoiding further disaster.

They are known for telling "little white lies" and sometimes some big ones, because experience has taught them that bending the truth or avoiding it has been the surest way out of danger. This becomes habit-forming, part of the automatic-reaction pattern when dealing with anything threatening. Yet they tend to judge themselves without mercy, not a surprising practice since they have almost never felt the pleasure of reward. Such a tightly-wound individual is not always pleasant to be with because life is too serious a problem with never-ending complications.

To say the least, they have grave difficulty in intimate relationships, having felt the terror of abandonment on a regular basis, and obviously they cannot trust but instead have an insatiable need for approval and affirmation. Working with people on the job or in other cooperative efforts is difficult in that they have no idea what to expect from the other people; they must guess at what the reactions of others might be. Nonetheless, they try extremely hard to please and remain very loyal to relationships.

If ever they find a relationship that works, it is a treasure to be worried about and protected at all cost. However, some have managed to develop a "science" of knowing how to please even the most impossible people and will do so endlessly at great cost to their own personhood.

Abuse at School

Sexual Harassment

Child abuse occurs in school with alarming frequency. Some 25 percent of females and 10 percent of males in grades eight through eleven have admitted to being sexually harassed by a teacher or some other member of school faculty (Shakeshaft, 1995). Tamara Elaine Shulman (1995) writes,

> When a child is molested or sexually abused, his or her innocence has been unjustly stolen. Such a child is scarred for life once he or she has been violated by anyone, especially if that person is a teacher—a person who deserves a child's respect and trust.
>
> Unfortunately, teachers who molest children in schools are depriving them of their natural instincts to trust. Without trust, a student-teacher relationship is impossible. If a child puts his or her trust in a teacher, a bond is created. That bond is fragile, and if broken, it causes children to re-evaluate the trust they have already placed in other individuals they care about.

Elementary-age children, being in Erikson's industry versus inferiority stage, are trying to realize basic competencies—to compete, and to excel. But the true self is entering subordination according to my model, and the false self is gaining influence. The illusion of power is carrying the child through this mild confusion and motivating him to continue exploration of self.

Abuse at this stage increases the momentum of the takeover by the false self as critical messages are conveyed: "You cannot trust; your power is gone; look at what Teacher did to you against your will; something wrong or bad in you caused this to happen." Further, even though the child will sense powerlessness, in conflict with his illusion of power, his or her illusion of power may be increased, for sexual abuse conveys to the child a long-lasting message that there is power in sex: power to control other people, even authorities.

Here is yet another reason that a girl, for example, may exhibit seemingly promiscuous behavior in adolescence and early adulthood: There is real power in sexuality, and this power comforts the haunting sense of helplessness.

Psychologist David Finkelhor (1986), an established authority on child abuse, has studied the results of schools that have instituted classes to teach children what sexual abuse is. He has found, in interviewing over 2000 school children, that children have a much easier time telling someone about being abused (no matter who the offender is) when they are in a supportive workshop environment. The feeling of safety in opening up is increased when the children hear stories of what others have been through.

Insult as Control

Far more common than sexual abuse in schools is the use of insult either in order to control students' behavior or as a means of venting frustration. Decades ago, teachers routinely paddled or whipped misbehaving children. Verbal putdowns and threats were not required. Today, there is a general, if not airtight, prohibition against corporal punishment of any kind in the classroom, and teachers are increasingly frustrated by not having a suitable way to control their students.

Greater creativity needs to be applied to the control of school children without either corporal or other punishment.

There are ways to apply discipline without damaging the child's image, especially when it is strongly emphasized that punishment and worth are not related. The message needs to be kept clear that certain behaviors have their own consequences and that the child has the power to control the behavior.

Recently I evaluated an 11-year-old black girl at her home, in the presence of her 10-year-old brother and their loving, doting grandmother. Both children had been raised with a strong value system that included loving and respecting themselves and other people. Their experiences in school had been uneventful for the most part until the present school year.

The girl had been on a school bus loaded with other children, almost all of them black. The driver had returned the children from another location back to the school because of noisy behavior on the part of the group. When the bus arrived, the white principal boarded the bus and, in anger, called them all "niggers".

This girl had never heard that term used before in such a way, and she was not sure of its meaning, although she knew it was bad. She had thought that the word pertained to anyone who was irresponsible, lazy, or stupid.

Only when she got home and talked to her grandmother did she discover that the word is what some white people call black people.

The interpretation was that she was a nigger, with every negative connotation. Her reaction was not rage, not defiance, not protest, but shame. She looked away as she related this incident, and there were tears in her eyes, but with the complete absence of any hostility toward the principal or anyone else.

Her brother added that he had been called the same name by the same principal twice, once when no one knew that he had overheard the comment. His interpretation and his reaction were similar to his sister's.

The children's illusion of power, rightfully belonging to them at that developmental stage, had been stripped. What should have been a time of channeling their process of becoming was detoured to an acceptance of information that was completely false—a lie. The subordination of self was accelerated as the false self took on more solid identity based on the lie.

A 7-year-old boy was referred for evaluation regarding another type of school abuse: He had been taped to his classroom chair all day for weeks at a time and was forced at other times to face the wall all day long. The teacher had said the punishment was due to his not sitting still. These outrages had occurred when the child was a kindergarten student.

I found him to be lethargic and depressed, plus lacking in normal spontaneity and sense of play. He was overly obedient, complacent, still, and quiet. His predominant affect was shame. This small boy had received information about himself by a mother substitute: his teacher, whose job it is to nurture and encourage.

The child's knowledge level was grossly below his demonstrated intelligence. It was obvious that he had basically stopped learning. Since a previous, independent examination by a child psychiatrist had ruled out a learning disability, it could only be concluded that this arrest of his learning process was the result of abuse, in school. His pre-school teacher had related that before he entered kindergarten, he was a keen and bright child, full of curiosity, who loved to learn. But at age 7, he was not able to name all of his colors, was slow in naming those he could, was able to count only to 29, and was not able to name the usual geometric shapes.

If we were to look at this child's condition, both in terms of learning theory and behaviorism, it would be easily seen that his natural inclination to explore his environment had been extinguished through repeated punishment and through sensory deprivation. The child had given up.

Misdiagnosis of Behavior

In the school systems, one of the most far-reaching and deeply damaging forms of abuse is the misdiagnosis or non-diagnosis of children's learning or behavioral problems. There is a critical need to understand the *root cause* of a child's academic difficulties rather than performing only standardized tests and then assigning the child to a broad, general category, such as SLD (slow learning disability), EH (emotional handicap), and ADHD (attention-deficit, hyperactivity disorder).

In addition, once the etiology of the problem is diagnosed, recommendations must be given so that the child can overcome (at least to some extent) any disability through a treatment plan specifically tailored to the needs of the individual. Such a plan should focus not only on limitations but on maximizing intact cognitive functions. There is little if any individualization in forming the child's IEP (individualized educational plan).

In the school systems I have dealt with, in Florida and South Carolina, there is little or no effort made to discover *why* a child has a difficulty. The "why" is covered over with a label.

Very, very often, with children as well as adults, my first job as a therapist is to remove a label that just doesn't fit. I see more misdiagnoses than accurate ones. As stated previously, a child's behavior and feelings both depend on what he's living with at home. Since there is no normal way to react to craziness, any adjustment is a maladjustment; hence, the development of symptoms and the consequent label.

Other times, the diagnosis is so incomplete as to be useless. An attorney I have worked with found it necessary to bring a lawsuit against the entire city in order to acquire a diagnosis and a treatment plan for his son. The school system insisted that these tasks had been accomplished. Their diagnosis was "anoxia"—not a diagnosis at all, but an event (oxygen deprivation). The diagnosis lies in what effect the anoxia had on the child's development. This is equivalent to a diagnosis of "football" when the condition is a broken arm.

In schools, as in the case with this child, students are almost never evaluated neuropsychologically. Brain damage, whether localized or global, is not considered. It is therefore impossible to determine which cognitive functions can be maximized and which can be somewhat improved, if possible.

In the case of emotionally handicapped children and adolescents, it has been my strong belief for 28 years that these disturbances are not "self-contained" and free-standing in the manner of medical conditions. They do not rise up from nowhere. For one thing, a child is a "barometer" reflecting his life experiences at home. Therefore, without being intrusive, the family system and the home environment must be comprehended adequately. If, for a time, a child has performed well but then begins to exhibit difficulties, something in the child's life has changed. But this obvious fact is not addressed in any sufficient manner.

Millions more dollars are poured out on school systems every year as politicians make new promises to improve education. They seem to believe that if they improve buildings, construct more buildings, pressure teachers into advanced education, establish merit systems, etc., then the system will produce a better "product".

The major question to be addressed, instead of all of these palliative approaches, is not why teachers cannot teach, but why students cannot learn. Most of the answers lie at home, not within the school walls.

One seasoned psychologist I know applied as an educational psychologist in a particular school district. The senior psychologist met with him and made it clear that he would not want such a job. She said, "All we do is test and then assign to special-education classes. Test and assign, test and assign." The applicant looked elsewhere for employment.

An experienced middle-school teacher has found that both she and her colleagues have lost complete control of the classroom. She has found it impossible to teach in the usual way because of chaos ruling at all times: students fighting, yelling, throwing, running around, and other confusion. There is no way that she can make them behave. Her solution is to take her portable radio to work, and sit at her desk with earphones always on.

There are a few students in the room who are trying against these odds to acquire an education. When one of them approaches her desk, the teacher puts down the earphones and instructs, one individual at a time.

These eager students are being abused by the administration. Children who will not behave or accept discipline should not be allowed to attend school. The educational setting should be exclusively devoted to those students who are willing to learn, or at least willing not to interfere with the learning of others.

The vast majority of teachers are very capable of teaching well. They are not the problem. The crisis is that they are unable to do their jobs. The solution is not more money thrown at the problem but a resolve on the part of school administrators, law enforcement, and the legislature to change the school environment.

Three brothers were all independently told by their irresponsible principal that they were not "college material". Not coming from a wealthy family in a class-conscious school, the boys had been excluded by other students from the circles of influence where wealth, social standing, and academics were valued. They were relegated to the "lower" classes of friends not only by students but also by teachers who adhered to the school's class system.

Fortunately, each boy had sufficient sense of self to ignore his high-school experience. One is today the vice-president of a large banking conglomerate, the second is the youngest full partner on record in the world's largest accounting firm, and the third is a doctor.

Many adolescents, as well as younger children, however, are not as fortunate. They make an estimation of their intelligence, motivation, and general capacity based on the strong opinions of teachers, other school personnel, and classmates. Many make determinations as to their worth as people, again based on unreliable information which is, most tragically, the only information available.

In the middle-school and high-school years, abuse occurs at the hands of other students as they discover experimental identities in cliques and systematically exclude other children who do not meet the criteria for membership. At a time when the young person is searching for an identity that might work in society—that is, experimentally "becoming"—the peer group brandishes the weapon of exclusion. The peers can make a "leper" out of a child who doesn't fit their standards.

Again, this is an administrative challenge. Principals and counselors, as well as teachers, know about the cliques. They should be discouraged and replaced with efforts to build a school-wide identity. Clique members should be addressed individually and made to understand how damaging their groups are to those excluded from them. Members of such groups also cheat themselves, for they acquire a group identity rather than develop further as individuals.

The reality is, however, that if a child's clothes bear the wrong label, or if he misses a sudden style change, he can become a pariah. The same can happen if he is too heavy, too thin, or in any way not resembling the always changing criteria for acceptance. One boy attending an upscale prep school wore a jacket that had the exact look of being in style but had the "wrong" label. Other students ripped the jacket off his back and tore it to shreds.

Covering It Up

There is a great deal of cover-up in the operation of schools. When children are attacked by other students repeatedly, the administration, plus the teachers obeying the administration, will deny that such incidents are occurring. The same lawyer I spoke of earlier found it necessary to sue the system for his child's protection. Security officers, on duty always, are required to report violence, but they do not always comply because the main part of their jobs is to prevent the violence from occurring. An incident is a "black mark" against the officer and the administration.

Ideally, school-district superintendents and school principals should hold the primary accountability for all of the problems discussed above. Unfortunately, the administrative education and training for such jobs is unlike those in industry. Qualifications are severely lacking.

Many are promoted school teachers who have never managed any group other than a classroom. In one school district in Florida, a retired Navy officer was hired as superintendent of an enormous system, even though he knew no more about education than the students and had never managed any organization except for his own Naval command.

8	# Neglect and Rejection

Researching Neglect

This section relies heavily on the pioneering and masterful work of Martha Farrell Erickson and Byron Egeland (1996), researchers in the Minnesota Mother-Child Interaction project.

Their research project, begun in 1975, traces the development of children identified before birth as being at high risk for neglect. The key factors used to classify the nearly 300 children as being at risk for poor developmental outcomes were poverty; early age of mother (mean, 20); low maternal education; marital instability or absence of marriage (67 percent); and stressful life circumstances. The authors write:

> While the bruises and scars of physical abuse are more readily apparent, the quiet assault of neglect often does at least as much damage to its young victims... and sometimes neglect just slowly and persistently eats away at the child's spirit until she has little will to connect with others or explore the world...

Out of the total sample of 267 children, 44 were physically abused, neglected, abandoned, or otherwise mistreated during the first two years of life. Of these, 24 were identified as neglected: Their parent(s) did not adequately provide for physical needs, the home environment was often unsafe, and the children were not adequately supervised.

Nineteen mothers were identified as "psychologically unavailable", meaning unresponsive to their children, failing to provide nurturance, comfort, positive responses to children's efforts at gaining attention, and not interacting with or showing interest in their child.

At 42 months, the neglected children were rated low on self-esteem and self-assertion, as well as ego control, flexibility, and creativity. They were withdrawn, easily frustrated, and lacking in persistence and enthusiasm, the authors report.

The neglected children had difficulty coping as they went through preschool. They were more dependent than children in the control group; scored lower in learning skills; and were developmentally delayed. In early elementary school, the children displayed severe problems in a number of areas, including attentiveness, involvement, self-reliance, and creativity. They were impatient, disrespectful, anxious about school work, and likely to make irrelevant responses in the schoolroom. They were seen as both aggressive/ acting out or as passive/withdrawn.

Further, the neglected children showed poor emotional health, lack of social competence, and increased attention-seeking. They had extreme difficulty adjusting to kindergarten. By 6th grade, all had been referred for special help, and 58 percent had been retained in their first two years of school.

"The failure of a child's caretaker to provide the necessary emotional responsiveness has devastating consequences on the early development of the child... Most disturbing was the sharp increase in the number of anxiously attached children from the 12 to 19-month assessment. Whereas at 12 months, 44 percent of the children in the psychologically unavailable group were anxiously attached, by 18 months, none of the children in this group was securely attached.

Clearly, the failure to nurture the infant emotionally resulted in the infant's resorting to a coping style that was a pattern of avoiding emotional contact, as if "I'm going to reject her before she can reject me again."

The authors state that by 54 months, factors such as aggressiveness, noncompliance, defiance, and disrespect were prevalent. They caused class disturbances and were described as unpopular, nervous and overactive. The problems continued in sixth grade, and the children were described by teachers as withdrawn, unpopular, inattentive, and low in achievement.

> Some investigators would disagree with our findings and argue that some children are not adversely affected by maltreatment. The reason some investigators have failed to find effects for all maltreated children is that they assessed development at one point in time rather than longitudinally, and assessed a narrow band of functioning (e.g., anger) rather than comprehensive assessments based on the salient developmental issues of a particular age.
>
> We found different patterns of maladaption at different ages. Many of our neglected children had difficulty coping in school; some lacked competence; some were angry; and some had low IQs. The patterns of maladaption were not identical; however, all showed ill effects in some area of development,

and by the time they were of school age, the effects were severe."

Using my own terms, these children were robbed of their right to express and explore their true selves through social interaction, mainly with Mother. Their false self was hastened in its arrival due to the nature of the conclusions a child draws about himself when ignored: "I don't exist. I don't count." They were denied the opportunity for their imaginary becoming, because no efforts paid off; and their taste of power was obliterated.

Rejection

While neglect is certainly a form of rejection, there are some children who are raised in fierce, open, and active discarding by a parent. Here, there is no subtlety. Some adults have never gotten over the vivid image of a father's icy stare signifying hateful contempt for the very personhood of the child. This kind of clear and total rejection is never fully overcome but can be carried, scars and all, if the true self is developed sufficiently through intensive, insight-oriented therapy aimed at throwing off the lies communicated during childhood.

In one of the most extreme cases I have treated, a widower with a 5-year-old son, Luke, married a woman who had not been married before and had no children of her own. From the very start, she became irritated by almost everything the boy did or said, even though the child had a very gentle and sweet personality and was very obedient. This little one, having his real mother's death still weighing on him, endured constant nagging and direct verbal abuse by his stepmother.

With each new child born to the couple, the rejection of Luke became worse. Stepmother eventually stopped pretending; quit hiding her hostility, even when visitors were present in the home. In time, anyone could see that she blatantly "had it in" for the boy. By the time he reached his teens, he tried to stay away from home as much as possible.

A very bright child, he lost all motivation; became a substandard student; gave up the career dreams and fantasies of his earlier childhood; and began to settle for existence rather than life. Luke was convinced that he deserved nothing. Even his father had given up any emotional support and gave all of his attention to the later children, those he shared with his wife. One day, when she was sure the boy would be away, the stepmother took everybody else to the photographic studio for a family portrait.

It happened that one night, as a young adult, this same victim, Luke, had managed to spend some time with his father, and the two had gotten very drunk. He used the occasion to ask the question that had plagued him all of his life: "Why did you never love me?" The father looked at him and said nothing as the son implored him again and again to answer. No answer ever came—not that night, not ever.

The son could not adjust to this horrible reality.

Processing the information, grieving, and moving on would be impossible until the condition made some kind of sense. He performed his own therapy by never giving up his search for a cause. Then, one day, through a distant family member, he received his answer: The man he thought was his father all of his life was not. He further learned that his deceased mother had been extremely promiscuous all during the marriage, and any one of a long list of men could be his real father.

Compared to the rejection issue, the identity of his biological father did not matter very much. Luke had solved his problem, for now there was an explanation. From the very instant of his discovery, he was relieved. Little grieving was necessary, because he had indeed mourned the issue all of his life. Now he knew the problem was not with himself. He became somewhat empowered, and very soon began the work of exploring who he really was, apart from being anyone's son. Very essential to him was a strong spirituality that enabled him to put the matter largely to rest by concluding that he was on Earth because his heavenly Father willed that he be here, and further, that there was an excellent purpose for his life.

Some children experience the brunt of rejection even when they are, in fact, loved. There are many parents who are quite able to love but not able to demonstrate it because of their own deficiencies in the way they were raised. A parent who has missed a warm, accepting, and openly affectionate relationship with his own parent can be disabled in what would be normal parent-child interaction. But such unfortunates are not aware of the deficiency because most people feel that what occurred in their families of origin was normal. Thus this "partial parenting," without intervention, will be passed on from one generation to another and will tend to produce "robotized" adults.

The best example I have ever witnessed of a father-son relationship was that of our neighbors across the street in the suburbs of Philadelphia. The time was long before I had even begun to study psychology; so I was concerned at all the affection that Tom showed for his son, Tommy, then about 9 or 10. Tom often picked him up without warning and kissed him on the cheek, pull him up on his lap, and stood with his arm around the boy, all to the point where I thought he would make his son into a "sissy". But I never commented on my opinion. In fact, Tom and I became very close friends.

As the years went by, I saw Tommy becoming more and more masculine, with the affection between father and son remaining very much in force. One night, when the boy was about 14, I was seated in their very large living room when Tommy came down the stairs. He looked around the room, saw several vacant seats, walked straight over to his father and sat down on his lap, as though that was his usual seat. Tom had been talking at the time, but never missed a word as he finished what he was saying.

Tommy became a man in the fullest sense, because Tom had passed on his own masculinity to the boy every time he delivered affection. The child's "welcome to manhood" had always been fully extended.

Rejection is, however, the strong message children receive when they are blamed for their parents' marriage problems. Many are told that "If it weren't for you kids, your father and I would never fight." Children, of course, take this information at face value and internalize it as valid. They may not realize how absurd the claim was until they become married and experience the reality that children are not the cause of marriage problems. In fact, and tragically, some children are born with the assignment of saving their parents' hopeless marriage in a last-ditch effort before divorce.

A child can suffer rejection because he reminds Mother (or Father) of herself, when Mother is furious with herself or seems to hate herself. The child might, alternatively, trigger memories of a hated or feared relative. At a time when the child is just being himself, he can receive a glare or a shout of correction for no apparent reason. Such children might actually be told directly, "You're just like your Aunt Ruth," or something similar. Again, the child absorbs the comment as fact about himself.

Too often, little girls are molested by their fathers, but more often by stepfathers. Many a mother will blame the child in order to preserve a positive regard for her mate. Mother has probably married such a man due to her own history. Since the child innately already believes that the atrocity is her fault, Mother's not believing her or, worse, blaming her casts in concrete the child's conclusion that she is herself bad.

Typically, the child will be so obsessed with the subject of her own sexuality that she will experiment lavishly in adolescence, as previously discussed. She will think sexually, feel sexual, and act sexual in the misdirection that her process of becoming has taken. Her taste of power and her illusion of power will be sexually based.

It is therefore no wonder that she will give off enough sexual energy to attract one or more predators. Thus, it is typical for molested little girls to be raped later in life. The rape obviously drives the foundation even deeper that her whole being consists of sexuality; that is, bad sexuality. Because she is bad, she is unworthy of decent companionship and is thus amenable to forming a partnership with an abusive male. In her mind, she deserves no better. When the abuse of that first significant relationship becomes intolerable, she will seek another partner, only to find him more abusive than the first.

Some girls will make a career out of sex as a dancer or a prostitute, with each dance or each "trick" confirming still further her sexual being and her badness. Many turn to drugs or alcohol, and most get arrested repeatedly, with the arrests by now not mattering because this condemnation by society fits well with the fully developed false self. Any illusion of power is long gone, except for sexual power, but that power is bad. All hope for "becoming" has long been given up.

It also happens in the opposite reaction too: the girl who rejects all sexuality, and disguises herself as physically unattractive.

The worst example of rejection that has come to my attention is addressed by M. Scott Peck (1983). He cites a case study in which the parents of a boy who had committed suicide by shooting himself gave the same gun to their other son as a Christmas gift. In his best-selling book, *People of the Lie,* he establishes the reality of literal evil in human beings. Among the characteristics of such people are several that have been confirmed over and over in my practice: 1) Evil people present an air-tight facade of being good; 2) they never admit being wrong, and 3) the people closest to them suffer major emotional damage.

An example is the mother described earlier who told her anorexic daughter that if the girl could get over it, "I can die in peace." While it would be comforting to think that it is both natural and universal for parents to love their children, experience dictates otherwise. There are some parents who hate their children, and the ones most suspect are those who try to possess their offspring for their own purposes, forever.

9 Domestic Abuse

Recently I addressed a county mental health association in a small South Carolina town. I began with the same startling sentence I had used on other occasions: "Domestic violence begins at 4." The doctors and nurses, though silent, were indeed puzzled as I scanned their faces. Because every child blames herself for the abuse or neglect she has suffered, the "my fault" message, deeply internalized, navigates the individual throughout life. Abuse, once begun, takes on a life of its own and finds people and occasions throughout life to multiply itself.

The abused little girl becomes the abused adolescent, who becomes an abused adult. Just as water seeks its own level, so an abused person seeks relationships and a lifestyle that are no better than what she believes she deserves.

Abusive men seem to have an uncanny intuition in being able to identify a girl or woman they can victimize. They can spot her a block away. Once they have their claws into her, they never let go. Even when a domestic violence victim gathers enough strength and support in a shelter to leave her present captor, she is not rid of him, because he follows, he stalks, and he torments from a distance in any way he can.

The Mennonite Domestic Violence Task Force (Lehman, 1996) has assembled 16 traits of an abuser that my own patients have studied in amazement. They are incredulous at the fact that their own tormentor fits this description so closely. Items 17 onward are derived from my own observations through treating abused women.

Signs of the Abuser

1. He is jealous and tries to "own" his partner.
2. He blames others for his faults.
3. He blames circumstances for his difficulties.
4. He demonstrates unpredictable behavior.
5. He belittles his partner verbally and tries to convince her she's crazy.
6. He cannot control his anger.
7. He always asks for another chance.
8. He promises and swears to change.
9. He says he was abused as a child or witnessed his father bully his mother.
10. He plays on his partner's guilt. ("If only you loved me, you would...")
11. His behavior often worsens when he uses alcohol or drugs.
12. He is closed-minded. His way is the only way.
13. He may seem charming and gentle to non-family members and the outside world.
14. He dislikes women, believes that a "woman's place is in the home," and that men have a right to possess women.
15. He may abuse his (or her) children by insult, intimidation, yelling, threatening, or physical violence.
16. He either refuses treatment, saying "You're the problem," or accepts treatment but plays games with the therapist.
17. He expects his partner to pay her own way financially.
18. He does not believe his partner when he asks where she's been.
19. He forces her into sex and other behaviors that she does not want.
20. He acts as though all income is his.
21. He threatens suicide or to kill her if she tries to leave.
22. He prevents her from making friends and/or engaging with her family.
23. He belittles her achievements and sabotages her accomplishments by insult.
24. He convinces her that he is doing her a favor by keeping her.
25. He either threatens violence or carries it out, or both.
26. He forbids her to make decisions on her own.

27. He repeatedly hammers away at her incompetence.
28. He belittles her friends and/or family.
29. He is unpredictable and undependable as a provider, often putting all responsibility for income on his partner.
30. He continues to stalk, harass, threaten, and frighten her in cunning ways, even when an injunction for protection has been issued.

Regarding item 9, in my own experience, men who have been abused as children are less likely, not more, to abuse women. While some studies tend to uphold item 9, they are based on men who are known abusers and who blame the fact on their childhood. Blaming others is a chief characteristic of an abuser. People who have been abused, whether male or female, tend to be compassionate, sensitive, and perceptive people.

Item 30, referring to a court-ordered injunction, bears special mention because police departments generally do not enforce such injunctions and often do not even serve them. In my work with an attorney in a major southern city, it was necessary to sue the sheriff's office in order to have an injunction served and enforced. The attorney and I underwent threats and intimidation by the police while the lawsuit was underway. The attorney's home was broken into, and his 90-year-old grandmother was threatened.

In every state, an injunction for protection is a court order, and it is the law for police to enforce the order. However, at this writing, many police departments were permitted to make their own decision as to whether to serve such an injunction or not. It was left to the discretion of the individual police officer what action to take, if any.

Domestic violence shelters routinely walk the victim through the process of obtaining an injunction, with the result being false security. They are not warned that the injunction may further enrage the abuser and place the victim in further, immediate danger.

A major exception is the State of Massachusetts, which has revamped its traditional ways of responding to domestic abuse. (AOL News Bulletin, February, 1999). Whenever a police officer has reason to believe that a person has been abused, or is in danger of being abused, the officer must use all reasonable means to prevent further abuse. By law, the officer is required to remain on the scene until there is no longer a threat of danger; assist the abused person in obtaining medical treatment; and help the victim get to a safe place. The officer must give the abused a notice of his or her rights and, if necessary, facilitate an emergency judicial response system now in place.

The officer is required to arrest any person when probable cause indicates that a domestic abuse prevention order has been violated.

These changes have come about at a time when wives have remained the most frequent victims of family murders for at least six years at this writing

(U.S. Dept. of Justice, 1994), and the incidents of horror continue to rise. Following a study of more than 8,000 homicides in large urban counties, the Bureau of Justice Statistics reported that a male is the assailant in about two-thirds of family murders. According to the study, 56 percent of the murderers had been previously convicted of other offenses.

Only a woman programmed by abuse all her life would marry such a man.

Abuse against women should be treated as a global health problem, according to a sweeping report that states at least one of every three women has been beaten, raped, or somehow mistreated. The Associated Press (1999), reporting on a study conducted by the Johns Hopkins School of Public Health and the Center for Health and Gender Equity, says the study is the first to take a close look worldwide at the subject. The report, "Ending Violence Against Women" (Heise, 1999), said that abused women suffer from depression and physical problems, and their children are more likely to be stillborn or die in infancy.

"Most of this stuff has never seen the light of day," said co-author Lori Heise, who visited some 20 countries during the past decade to collect data from some 2,000 other studies of domestic violence. Between 22 and 70 percent of the women interviewed had never before told anyone about the abuse they had suffered. Beyond recent, visible injuries, abuse has now been linked to gastrointestinal disorders and chronic pain syndrome, as well as gynecological problems, complicated pregnancies, and substance abuse.

The report asserts that the healthcare system is the only institution that interacts with nearly all women during their lives, and that health professionals are in a unique position to identify and assist victims. "I see the healthcare setting as an opportunity," Heise states, but "...right now it's an opportunity lost."

Speaking to the Associated Press, Dr. John Nelson, a spokesman for the American Medical Association, said that a poll commissioned by the organization found that abused women would rather speak to their physician than to anyone else.

"Violence against women should be treated as a health issue, not just a legal matter," the report asserts. In Nicaragua, children of abused women were six times more likely to die before age 5, and women in India who had been beaten were more likely than others to face miscarriages, stillbirths, or infant deaths, Heise reports.

Why Women Stay

Why do women, especially in America, put up with these outrages? The main reason is obedience to the messages of childhood—that they deserve no better. Many people find it difficult to believe, but the greater the abuse, the greater is the obedience factor.

A very strange phenomenon occurred at the end of World War II. When the allied troops came to free the prisoners of war, when the fences were down and the captors in custody, some prisoners refused to leave the camp. They would huddle and resist being moved. It was found that the captors who had been most cruel, most sadistic, and most forceful had won the greatest loyalty of their captives. Thus, there is this dependable equation, which I have seen in hundreds of abused women: the greater the abuse, the greater the obedience.

It is my premise that the normal way for both children and adults to react to abuse is to obey the message it conveys. Herein lies the reason that victims are so resistant to change, even when competent therapy is provided. To disobey the message of the tormentor is akin to being a traitor.

Another factor is that terrifying abusers live as phantoms in the minds of their victims. Many an adult, woman or man, feels that the original abuser, and often the present abuser, is "living in their head." This almost magical presence living on in the mind of a victim is sometimes so acutely felt that it has a voice of its own that can be confused with a hallucination. The communication is always negative and condemning and is continuously repeating the original message that "you are no good; you are not a real person; you dare not try to do better."

The difference between this kind of "voice" and hallucinations is that the former is more in line with a constant flashback, or memory so vivid that the abuser can almost be heard; however, the victim knows that the voice is a reliving experience. Hallucinations, as they occur in schizophrenia, are believed by the patient to be as real as any other reality.

The child, or "true self," as I name it, can be thought of as having an impermeable layer of protection around it. Such might also be thought of as a boundary, or a wall, enclosing the self. The abuser, by attacking the personhood of his victim, continuously assaults this barrier until at last he breaks all the way through and "sets up residence" inside.

Prisoners of war experience the same sensation through brainwashing. The barrier of the self is weakened by the infliction of excruciating pain that continues beyond endurance. Combined with sleep and food deprivation, the pain is applied with dehumanizing insults, in some way implanting the same message, no matter what words are used: "You are nobody."

The brainwashing is complete when the tormentor has broken through and has begun to live inside the mind of the victim. This is the nature and the power of child abuse. It is brainwashing of the first magnitude, accomplished with greater ease because the subject is a child, without power. When done effectively, brainwashing conditions the victim to accept the role of captive permanently. Hence, in domestic violence, we do not have a new occurrence of a destructive relationship resulting from a poor choice or a mistake that anyone could make. We have a continuation of the same earlier brainwashing with one abuser continuing where the other left off.

Minor reasons that battered, insulted, overly controlled, or humiliated women do not leave include the following:

- Hope that the partner will change
- Partially believing that trying harder will make a difference
- Fear of what the partner may do in retaliation (a well-grounded fear, implying that the victim needs protection)
- Not knowing what to do about the children
- Lack of money
- Having no place to go
- Not knowing whom to call
- Thinking that nothing can be done
- Fear of living alone, without support
- Thinking the problem isn't that bad, after all
- Feeling the police and the courts won't help enough or fast enough (true in many cities)
- Religious and moral convictions
- Fear of the unknown.

A critical item to be added to the above list is that many women are not conscious of the fact that they are in an abusive relationship. Their life experience, with the internalized messages that define their self image, prevents them from recognizing how preposterous their situation is. For this reason, I have developed the checklist below.

This inventory, which has been administered to approximately 100 women known to have been abused by their partners, has yielded the consistent response: "I didn't know I was being abused until I took the test. I thought my relationship was normal but just had some problems."

Therefore, the intent is to help victims realize that they are in an abusive relationship. The inventory is for use by counselors, psychologists, psychiatrists, social workers, clergy, lawyers, physicians, police, child protection workers, and others, either to determine the likelihood of abuse or to convince the victim that she is indeed being abused, and thus break through the brainwashing described above.

It is my strong assertion that this checklist or one like it should be in the hands of all of the following, for very frequent usage:

- Emergency departments
- Rape crisis centers
- Domestic abuse shelters
- Courthouses—the department where women file injunctions for protection (usually under the State Attorney's office)
- Community mental health centers
- Drug and alcohol treatment centers
- Psychiatric hospitals and hospital departments of psychiatry
- City offices of victim services
- Women's advocacy groups
- Police departments
- Physicians' offices

Consequences of Staying

As they continue their subsistence in this type of prison environment, they face any of the following, as a consequence of staying:

- Further injury or death
- Depression
- Suicidal tendencies
- Increasing helplessness (illusion of powerlessness)
- Shutdown of everyday functioning
- Acute and chronic anxiety, often with panic attacks and/or agoraphobia
- Economic disaster
- Severe symptoms in children
- Social isolation
- Post-traumatic stress disorder (discussed at length later)

Because social isolation is a consequence, the woman is usually without a good-enough friend to help with a rescue operation; that is, to help her leave and provide what is necessary for housing, child care, and all the other requirements for breaking the cycle. As a result, many cities have established programs to perform these life-saving functions.

A problem with most programs is that they are used heavily by the economically and culturally deprived. Middle-class women are subjected to a culture shock when suddenly thrust into a milieu that is foreign to them. These shelters tend to have a "ghetto" atmosphere, and in some, the living conditions are deplorable.

These domestic violence projects usually assist victims in filing restraining orders against their oppressors. The victims feel somewhat comforted by such a court injunction until they find out that the piece of paper is worthless, as discussed previously. The victims receive group therapy by paraprofessionals and volunteers with an anti-male slant. Upper-level mental health professionals, such as psychologists and psychiatrists, are rarely associated with these havens except perhaps on a consulting basis. Few of these consultants, however, are familiar with the treatment of emotional trauma or any of the roots of domestic violence.

I mean no less than to say that many of these facilities are in the "Dark Ages" regarding what a victim needs. But these organizations, for the most part, are deeply entrenched in the community and not open to change, nor to the application of effective treatment by well-qualified professionals. They have staked out their territory, and they are not about to allow outsiders within their borders.

My friend the attorney, of whom I spoke earlier, joined me at a meeting of a domestic-violence task force. When he pointed out that injunctions were neither being served nor enforced, he was branded as a trouble-maker and barred from coming back. I was told that I could return if I did not interfere but to "keep that lawyer away from here."

A "model" facility, according to my view, would be headed by a full-time social worker or psychologist who has thoroughly studied child abuse, emotional trauma, and the treatment of both. As discussed later, the treatment of domestic violence is the treatment of child abuse for the most part, and it is always the treatment of emotional trauma, quite often post-traumatic stress disorder. This director would also have enough training in neuropsychology to diagnose traumatic brain injuries. In addition, an attorney with training and experience in abuse would be retained on a contract, on-call basis.

It is common knowledge that more than one-third of women who visit emergency departments are there for on-going abuse and that up to two-thirds of these victims are beaten while pregnant. Yet, the abuse is rarely reported. Further, the patients are "patched up" and released to return to their battleground.

Even though blows to the head and face cause most visible injuries, the likelihood of brain damage is not explored except in rare cases, and then only by electronic imaging. These diagnostic tools, such as MRIs, miss most types of brain damage, as do routine neurological examinations. The majority of brain injuries are detectable only through neuropsychological testing, which detect cognitive deficiencies. Hospitals, however, generally shun psychologists, so that they are rarely on staff to perform such evaluations, and they are not included as a referral source. Psychiatrists receive the referrals, if any are made, and they, in turn, are not familiar with neuropsychological diagnostics or else prefer not to resort to the expertise of a psychologist.

There are many exceptions to the exclusion of psychologists by hospitals, but the two professions of psychiatry and psychology do not generally work conjointly as logic would dictate. As a result, most of the head injuries occurring as a result of child and/or domestic abuse are not detected.

Brain Damage Symptoms

Contrary to fact, the myth remains that head injuries are caused only by an impact to some part of the head. Both psychologists and psychiatrists, when examining victims, should inquire about falls, unconsciousness, whiplash-type incidents, and anoxic events, to name only a few causes. Attorneys as well should ask these questions and many more. The following are not always symptoms of brain injury, but they can be, and a combination certainly warrants further procedures for a useful diagnosis:

- Memory loss
- Slowed thinking
- Pauses during questioning
- Vision or hearing changes, including double vision and tinnitus
- Dizziness
- Fatigue and sleepiness
- Loss of balance
- Difficulty communicating
- Headaches
- Misjudging distances
- Trouble understanding verbal communication
- Tremors, seizures, spasms
- Confusion
- Confabulation (making up stories)
- Trouble performing routine tasks
- Unusual gait
- Numbness or tingling, any part of body
- Decreased initiative
- Personality change
- Denial of an evident mental problem

- Agitation
- Anxiety and/or depression without a history of the same
- Impulsiveness
- Odd movements or behaviors
- Nightmares
- Social withdrawal
- Explosive rage (especially without recall)
- Chronic fatigue
- Self-centeredness
- Over-reaction to sudden noises or movements
- Loss of former interests

A recent patient of mine, Maggie, received such massive brain damage in a beating by her partner that she was not expected to live. She remained unconscious on life support for weeks. When she resumed consciousness, she was blind in one eye, she had lost her ability to speak, and her emotional control was severely affected. She would laugh at every question she was asked.

The mother of four children, Maggie had been a vibrant, energetic worker at her job, and was well-liked due to her delightful personality. Her injuries disabled her to the extent that she could not care for her children, so she and her children took up residence with her mother, who had severely abused her verbally throughout her life and who proceeded to scream at the children constantly. I had attempted to treat her at home, but the grandmother's screaming made this impossible. It was necessary to arrange special transportation so that she could come to my office.

Maggie remained in love with her batterer, and, for her own safety, had to be watched constantly so that she would not sneak back to see him. He had received a sentence of only six months in jail, but served only half of that.

An ideal shelter would care for both the mother and her children, but certainly not in an "institutional" environment as is mostly the case. The ambiance would be resort-like and would provide ample privacy. Instead of making the victims prepare their own meals and clean their own quarters, they would be "pampered" as guests who had earned the right to "royal" treatment through what they had suffered.

A family physician, a pediatrician, and a gynecologist would be on-call, contractually. Instead of riding in a van to a clinic, they would receive their medical care on-site. There would be a play area for children, well supervised by gentle staff. There might be an exercise room, but certainly a very pleasant social area, attractively and comfortably furnished. Each individual room would have its own bath and be equipped with TV, plush carpet, and other amenities.

One might say that the expense would be prohibitive. However, that is not the case, as professional fees would be covered by third-party payers, such as Medicaid, private insurance, or grant funding. The facility itself could be constructed with the help of an allocation of the city or county budget, or perhaps through private or corporate grants.

Specialized individual and group treatment would be available on a daily basis, including weekends, but attendance would be optional when first admitted. A full-time nurse who understands the issues and is perhaps a survivor would be a key staff member.

In brief, any connotation of punishment, "sentencing" or forced confinement must be completely reversed because, after all, the victim believes that she deserves punishment. That mindset is one of the first that must be countered.

Domestic Violence Inventory

1. Are you afraid of your partner?
2. Do you feel as though you have to "walk on eggshells" to keep your partner from getting grouchy?
3. Has your partner ever hit, slapped, or punched you?
4. Do you feel you deserve to be punished?
5. Do you ever have the feeling you've done something wrong but you don't know what it is?
6. Have you lost respect or love for your partner?
7. Are you ever afraid your partner will hurt the children?
8. Have you ever daydreamed of killing or disabling your partner?
9. Is your partner good to you most of the time but suddenly gets scary?
10. Are the children afraid of your partner?
11. Does your partner ever tell you you're crazy?
12. Has your partner ever threatened to hurt you?
13. Do you ever fear you may be seriously hurt by your partner?
14. Has your partner ever threatened to commit suicide?
15. Has anybody warned you to get out of the relationship?
16. Were you abused or neglected as a child?
17. Has your partner forced you to do things you don't want to do?
18. If you say "no" to your partner, is there danger?
19. Have you lost any friends due to your partner?
20. Does your partner have to approve where you go and when?
21. Have you lost a job because of your partner?
22. Does your partner stop you from doing things you want to do?
23. Does your partner doubt your word; that is, not believe you?
24. Do you feel emotionally numb?
25. Are you afraid to tell anyone what's really going on?
26. Have you ever wanted to call the police or someone else for protection?
27. Do you ever feel hopeless about your situation?
28. Have you ever thought about running away?
29. Does your partner change when using alcohol or drugs?
30. Are you forced into sex when you're not willing?

31. Do you feel like your partner's personal possession?
32. Have you ever been in a violent or controlling relationship before?
33. Was there bad fighting in the family you grew up in?
34. Are you a grown child of an alcohol or drug abuser?

Only a few positive answers to the above questions, perhaps only one, are required as an indication of possible seriousness. Contrary to the belief of the victim, most women do not live this way, and would not continue to tolerate any of the outright offenses included above. But victims tend to stay in their captivity, mainly due to obedience, as stated, to the early childhood messages.

10 | A Man's Account

Compared to domestic violence against women, the offense applied to men is rare but yet, not absent. Male victims of domestic abuse are rarely attacked physically; instead, they are more frequently assaulted verbally and mentally in partnerships. In my practice, I have treated both men and women, although in separate groups. Because the same dynamics apply for men; that is, child abuse leading to later abuse, it is worth devoting this account of one single case, because it is indeed an excellent example of the principles so far discussed.

David's story resembles my own in the very beginning. Since age 7, we both believed that our fathers wanted us dead. A horrible beating in second grade similar to mine but not as severe caused David to become terrified in his father's presence from that day on.

Before, when he was younger, David was always excited to see his dad come home. He used to watch for him to appear up at the end of the block and run to go meet him. He would get a great big welcome from Dad, and it was the best part of the boy's day.

Some time after the beating, while still in elementary school, David came to believe in God. But that only made things worse, because now there was someone even bigger and more powerful to keep at bay. So in order to avoid His wrath, the boy stopped whatever he was doing many times during the day and knelt down, then bent all the way forward to kiss the ground. This bizarre act became a "magical" way of keeping God from attacking him or his mother. He dared not stop the ritual, no matter how much the other children laughed at him. It was better to undergo complete humiliation many times every day than to take a chance. David had no imaginary power of his own; instead, the ritual held the power. He cannot remember how long that behavior continued, but he estimates it was more than a year.

He did not have any real interest in girls until he was 15. Even then, he preferred being with his friends, the guys he would explore the sewers with, go camping with, and watch late-night horror shows with. They were kids who did not fit in with the cliques at school. They were "in-betweeners": very intelligent but interested in nothing, fully capable of academic excellence but not considering college preparation, something that would be natural for them. They simply existed.

One day, in 10th grade, there was a girl with a very pretty face sitting across the table from David in their classroom. He was moved to speak to her, and to his astonishment, she spoke back in a warm, encouraging way. After a few dates, a problem arose. She said that she did not want to be with somebody with only a "D" average and on the verge of failing algebra. Delores was an honor-roll student. So David knew he had to start trying, even though he did not really believe that he could do any better.

As they continued to date, Delores seemed to build David's experimental self. She gradually, over many conversations, started to make him think that he was intelligent and even had a special mission in life—perhaps becoming a pastor or something (even though she made it plain that she would never marry a pastor).

Delores seemed to have serious problems with her parents and sisters. As she and David talked and caressed intimately, time after time, over the next two years or so, she made him think he was helping her. (Of course, he was not, because he was a child himself). But to him, his experimental power became laced with a sense of value. It was also very clear to him how much Delores needed him as well. The process led to mutual dependence, even though David felt the price was too high. In other words, she demanded all of his time and all of his attention. He was no longer "allowed" to be with any other friend. She, on the contrary, had complete freedom to be with anyone she wished, whenever she wished.

David recalls one time in the summer when Delores went with her family to the seashore and said he couldn't visit her there because she was going to try dating some other people. He was unaware then, but this condition had been set as a ploy to "pull him in deeper." He did not know that he was about to become possessed by her.

A merger had occurred, in David's mind, through plentiful sexual activity, not including intercourse. He had begun to feel part of her, and to have her go away into someone else's arms rocked him to his already shaky foundations. He stayed in his bedroom the whole time she was away and suffered agony beyond anything he has been able to put into words. He did not understand what was happening to him, and certainly could not explain it. All he knew was that he was living in both anguish and terror.

He says had that trial lasted much longer, he would surely have died. He had fantasies of being the lead character in the movie *The King and I*

(1956), who wasted down to his last breath. He still cries when he sees that movie.

Delores, of course, did come back, and was more demanding of his time and emotional energy than ever. Once, when David resisted one of her manipulations, she broke into violence and started hitting him with her little fists. Certainly she did not hurt him physically; on the contrary, he came to a moment of lucidity. He became almost empowered enough to break the relationship, but he caved in when she came to his house, hysterically begging him to take her back.

David managed to go to college in a distant city, with the heavy assistance of his parents, both of whom wanted to get Delores out of their son's life. He was happier there than he had ever been. But about halfway through the second semester of his freshman year, she employed the "seashore" scam and informed him that she was planning to date other people. Her daily letters had given hints of her attraction to other young men, although they were packed with expressions of passionate love for him. The double messages kept him constantly off-balance. Finally, he decided to transfer to the college she attended. Her strategy had worked perfectly.

They were married in their junior year. David, fed up with the mixed communications, insisted that they would either marry or break up for good. Actually, they did both. When David returned from work the very day after their brief honeymoon, he found that she had slammed a window on her hand repeatedly and had burned her arm with matches. She had also been sitting at the top of the fire escape and said she was debating whether or not to jump off.

She never did.

For the next 13 years, without a break, she kept David believing that she was suicidal. Of course, it became his job to make sure she did not kill herself. The impossibility of his assignment, combined with his concern for her and the absolute unpredictability of each day's events, constantly sabotaged his adopted self.

David was forced to go to work every day without knowing whether he would find his wife alive when he returned. When he came in the door each night, he had to search for her and often find her in a closet refusing to talk. Sometimes he would succeed in getting her out of the closet, and sometimes he would not. When he did, she would parade around either topless or completely nude and then become furious when he wanted to touch her. The only time they had sex was when she decided she wanted to have a child. Then, when she did not get pregnant immediately, she became more "suicidal."

He took her to a psychologist, then a psychiatrist, then another psychiatrist, and in the 13th year, a family therapist. The last course of therapy led to her becoming addicted to both alcohol and prescription drugs, and the "therapy" climaxed with her running away, carrying a stash of pills, alcohol, and an antique pistol David's father had given him. After that event, the therapist refused to see her anymore.

It was just as well, because Delores had never talked—not at all—with any of the doctors she had seen. In all, David had committed her to lock-up psychiatric facilities four times, once with the assistance of her own mother. It was either commit her or allow the chance that she might carry through her suicide threat. Only recently has David, now a middle-aged man, realized that his wife had numerous opportunities to kill herself but never did. She killed David—at least his adopted self.

In this 13-year nightmare, David discovered a friend, not in the form of a person, because he was permitted no friends, but in the form of alcohol. He had always enjoyed his drink at lunch and his martinis before dinner, all part of normal living, according to the way he had been raised. But about two years into the marriage, he found that a morning drink, before he left for work made it so much easier to leave. He also discovered that the same procedure, before coming back at night, greatly dulled the experience of hunting for his wife.

He had long ago given up on God and the church people he had known. Neither God nor the people ever showed up to help him, or even called. He vividly recalls pleading beyond pleading for God to help Delores during her "attacks", but no help ever came. Alcohol, however, always worked.

Over the years, alcohol began to fill in the missing parts of his adopted self and to replace the wife he thought he should have some relationship with. His new friend—alcohol—filled the voids for years.

After these 13 years, Delores underwent a "spiritual experience" and claimed that she had spent the day with Jesus. She quit cold-turkey all the medicine she had been consuming daily, along with the alcohol she had drunk in enormous amounts. Then she demanded that David stop.

David had no intention of giving up the only friend he had ever been able to depend on. The more she pressured him, the more fearful he became of being forced to give up his remedy. The effect was that his drinking increased, but in secret.

Periodically, Delores caught him, either by smell or the way he acted. Then he had to beg her forgiveness and swear never to drink again. But he continued drinking alcoholically for more than five years after she had stopped.

Eventually David had to try to stop for his own sake. A friend of his, who was a physician, found that his liver was two-and-a-half times normal size; that his pancreas was malfunctioning; that certain reflexes were gone. The doctor said he would be dead in six months unless he quit immediately. But he could not stop. There was not enough left of David to rise to the task.

In the course of the marriage, the couple had four biological daughters. While pregnant with the fourth, Delores insisted on having a tubal ligation following the delivery. David hated the idea with a passion. He loved the children he had, and he believed that the procedure amounted to mutilation. Delores, backed by her therapist at the time, had the ligation anyway. By the time the youngest child was two or three, she began to complain bitterly that she could not have more children.

Soon after the youngest was 9, Delores wanted to adopt a baby with mixed racial background. David had no objection, and in fact welcomed the idea of another child. He realizes now that besides truly loving children, he had a hidden motive: that another child would keep his wife occupied.

She certainly needed something to occupy her. Ever since their first-born was 9 years old, Delores gave the children the responsibility of housekeeping, eventually including preparation of meals. She herself did nothing except for projects that amused her for a time. When she was in her early 20s, she worked for a month or so at a children's shelter, but quit when she became pregnant. Early in that pregnancy, she was "suicidal" because she thought she was not pregnant.

Back to David's alcoholism. He managed to stay sober on one stretch for 10 straight years. But up until five-and-a-half years ago, he had been detoxified, near death, four times. Each "slip", however, lasted only a few days before he turned himself in.

By adopting a second newborn daughter, again with mixed racial background, the couple became the parents of six daughters: four biological, and two adopted. The oldest four of the six are grown with children of their own. They remember their dad being drunk only a few times because he did not drink except during the brief relapses mentioned, and those did not last long.

What these daughters do not understand is that their father was not himself at any time during their formative years. They do not know that their father continued to live out the horrors of his life as a lost and incomplete person. They witnessed a personality, but not a person. It was not David, but his false self, his adopted self, that they grew up with.

David did not even begin a true discovery of his self until he gave up both alcohol and his wife for good. His final detoxification triggered what was to become a gradual realization of all the lies he had swallowed; all the manipulations he had endured; all the false guilt he had harbored.

The last binge, as David now knows, was a veiled suicide attempt. He was hoping that he would never wake up, that he had consumed a lethal amount of alcohol. When he awoke in the detoxification facility, he paced the hall relentlessly until a nurse gave him a shot. He was in a state of nauseating depression, unbearable remorse, terror, and absolute helplessness. He wanted with everything in him to die, and as soon as possible.

He doesn't know whether anyone has ever wanted to die more than he did; but there was no way out, as usual. Not even death was an option, because he had let his life insurance lapse, and if he died, the family would have no income. He knew Delores would never work, and even if she did, she could never earn the income needed for their family. So here David was: a man with no life in him but forced to live.

The loudspeaker in the hall squawked that an Alcoholics Anonymous (AA) meeting was starting and that everybody had to attend. David sat down with the other men, dressed in pajamas and foam slippers, and then listened to the meeting begin. Then a strange thing happened. It occurred to him that maybe there was one more hope: that after all these years, this program of recovery might be able to teach him something that would finally work.

Later, while lying on his bed and staring at the paint peeling off the ceiling, while occasionally tracing a roach scurrying to find cover, he made a resolution. He committed himself to life, but it must be a very different life. David told himself that he had to change everything about his approach to living. He would put all of his beliefs, convictions, attitudes, desires—everything—up for scrutiny and a fresh look through the eyes of AA. He would become open-minded about every new idea he would encounter. He did not realize it then, but his first and most important task was to find the "real David".

Unfortunately, for him and countless others, AA did not help for long; in fact, he was eventually to find himself by finding his calling. Why Twelve-Step programs fall short is discussed in the chapters on treatment.

Up until now, David had lived in terms of other people: what they believed; what they needed; what would make them happy. He understood other people very well, and he knew that he had been given some sort of a gift for helping people. But never had he given the slightest thought to finding himself.

When he was discharged and returned home, he acquired from seemingly nowhere the freedom to disagree with some people he had never questioned before and conversely, to agree with some he had always been at odds with. Delores thought this was all a sign of instability—or maybe that's what she hoped. She had no idea that his eyes had been truly opened, and that he was not going back.

This new resolve, as stated, was the beginning of his getting well; that is, finding the truth about himself. He began to examine everything he had ever believed all over again, whether he had changed his mind on the subject already or not, and no matter how many times.

He found himself strongly disagreeing with Delores on various matters, especially child rearing, even though he had never dared before. He sensed that she had chosen a rut to remain in for the rest of her life and was not by any means going to join him in his life-enhancing adventure. Whether she came or not, he was on his way, for survival was the issue.

As time went on, David found he was angry at his wife most of the time, and vice-versa. He had begun to dread coming home from work, because even though she no longer hid in closets, she did not do much else either. But what bothered him the most was the way she treated their first adopted daughter, whom we'll name Amy. Delores, having become a fanatical, Pentecostal "Christian" years before, blamed demons for Amy's being a difficult child.

David realized that Amy had been a difficult child, but that Delores had always managed her in a wrong and sometimes crazy way, despite his protests. In fact, his objections only brought down the rage of his wife on both him and the child. So there had been no win.

One night, when the child was only four, David found her tied to a bookshelf by her pigtails, in which predicament the child was screaming and struggling desperately to get loose. Delores had said the child was full of demons and had the strength of ten men. David promptly untied her and comforted the child, despite his wife's fury.

About five years ago, when Amy was only ten, Delores returned to drinking, but only before dinner. She would get extremely mellow, to put it mildly; and then after dinner, which made the buzz wear off, she became vicious toward both David and the children, but especially Amy. This activity was during David's first year after detoxification. She drank in front of him, and he admits buying her the alcohol. He says taking the chance of going into a liquor store was worth the risk in order to earn a brief period of peace during Delores' mellow period before dinner.

During a very rare, heated encounter, David broke out with the words, "Shut the *f—* up!" Then he sprung on her the threat of divorce. Then he backed down and said he would work late and come home to see the children briefly before they went to bed; that he would sleep on the sofa, and see the children in the mornings before going to school. Delores insisted that he leave permanently. He did, that very night.

He says that leaving Delores was like leaving himself, for he hadn't known where he stopped and she began. He was unable to make himself go very far in distance, so he slept on the floor of his nearby office. His Twelve-

Step sponsor, as soon as he learned what had been happening, seized the opportunity to get David free before it was too late. For years, the sponsor and other friends from AA had warned him that his sobriety was at stake unless he got away from her.

The sponsor took him to his own home, with his wife and child. It had taken the sponsor about three hours to convince David to come with him. He did not want to venture too far from the prison camp, just like the soldiers in World War II. Indeed, the overwhelming feeling that tortured David was that of being the worst traitor in the world. In the next few months, David lost 20 pounds due to feeling too guilty to eat.

It is a fact that alcoholism very often—and perhaps most often—follows abuse, whether mental, sexual, or physical. The alcoholic is the ultimate living example of a false self trying to survive without any real power. Alcoholics Anonymous can affect the discovery of one's true personhood.

AA stopped making any difference for David as time went on. But he did eventually find that his own life was as important as anyone's—something he could never grasp before. He also, in time, underwent the revelation that he, and all of us, are supposed to be happy—that happiness, not misery, is the normal state of being.

David relates:

> The first thing to understand about God is that you can't understand God. You must accept this. The second thing to get right is that you need Him. The third thing is that you are not Him and you can't do his job. The fourth thing is that He is love. The fifth thing is that he is not a theologian.
>
> Today, if someone were to ask me to define God, I would say that I wouldn't dare. I can't even define a human being. It would be much easier for me to say what He is not. He is not the God of wrath and punishment that I always, at heart, thought He was. I was afraid of Him all of my life. So I made another 'god', out of alcohol.
>
> In all my religious pursuits, I have never experienced Him, only heard about Him through the various opinions of some famous and some not-so-famous people who thought they knew Him.

David had actually gone all the way back to adolescence and re-performed his developmental work regarding experimental identity and experimental power. His active participation in group therapy with other men began to give him an identity. Comments at meetings helped greatly in obtaining new and accurate information about himself.

The spiritual component of the group enabled him to find a father replacement, which he termed "God, my Father". The new father justified his existence, and his belief initiated a search for purpose in his life. This time, he knew that his "calling" was not to keep Delores alive, nor to make her happy. The new meaning of his existence, as opposed to his previous misconception, had to be possible.

Just as male batterers do, female abusers continue to punish the former captive through whatever means they can find. Delores has maintained her manipulation through the courts as the divorce, even at this writing, continues.

About two years after the separation, David was returning from a meeting one night when he saw Delores and Amy sitting in a car, waiting for him. They both approached, with Delores saying, "She's all yours. She's full of demons."

David was very happy about this surprise, because he loved his daughter very much, and he saw an opportunity to correct all the verbal, and sometimes physical, abuse Delores had put the child through. Amy was now about 12.

He was nowhere close to realizing that he had been presented with another impossible task. He was now in charge of an infuriated, defiant, and vicious child, so full of hate that her rage spread to everyone, but especially to David, because now he was in charge. Just as lightning tends to strike the tallest object, rage always strikes the closest person. David had no idea that he was to go through hell because of what Amy would do. He was about to experience how some children, who have a very strong constitution, react to abuse: through outrageous behavior. They pay back.

Amy had been abandoned by her birth mother, her adoptive mother, and when David left, her adoptive father. Her rage exploded everywhere, and the rampage was to last for years.

First, she began disrupting classes at school, then insulting teachers, then skipping school, then assisting in an apartment burglary, then running away for days at a time, then running away for weeks at a time, and finally running away for months at a time, taking haven in crack houses in the inner city. Her last long-term runaway was a full three months until she was picked up by police. She told the officers she had run away because her father had sexually abused her from the age of five.

Even though the officer from the sex crimes unit did not believe her, and in spite of the fact that the state attorney saw nothing in the case, the Florida Department of Children and Families drew up a petition for dependency anyway. The petition violated the legalities regarding hearsay exception rules, but the court accepted the petition and granted it totally without evidence of any kind.

As an aside, it should be stated that child protective services agencies violate the law most of the time in presenting their petitions for dependency. There is no due process for the accused, and there is no way an innocent person can escape. Once the petition is granted, the child becomes a ward of the state. If the agency cannot build a criminal case against the accused, he is denied the right to have any kind of contact with any minor children.

In a large city, best left unnamed, the county's juvenile court goes along with a scam between the agency and certain favored psychologists in private practice who make their living from agency referrals. In order for the accused ever to be able to have contact with his children again, he must be "evaluated" by one of these few psychologists. If the accused maintains his innocence, he is labeled "in denial" and in need of two years of weekly therapy. If he admits to the alleged offense in order to complete the process and see his children again, he is labeled a "sex offender" in need of weekly therapy until the psychologist discharges him.

David chose not to play the game. Thus, he cannot have contact either with Amy (wherever she is) or with his younger adopted daughter, and certainly not his wife.

Delores seized upon this opportunity as being too good to be true, and immediately began a prolonged effort of convincing their grown children that David had done the same to them, but they just do not remember. She pressured and threatened the state attorney to arrest her husband. In fact, she harassed the man so often that he contacted David and said, "Your wife is crazy." She also communicated the lie to the authorities governing David's profession, so that he was driven out of business. Then, when he fell behind in temporary alimony and child support, she tried to have him arrested for failure to pay.

What did the most damage to David was the fact that there is no way to disprove such an allegation. He believed that all of his children had a seed planted in their minds that he might actually be a pervert. Thus, he found it impossible to face any member of his family.

David deteriorated. Loss of his profession meant loss of a substantial part of his identity. Loss of his family was too much to bear. The threat of going to jail for unpaid child support was the final straw. He tried to kill himself.

He survived by a very narrow margin, and was then committed by the emergency department to a public psychiatric holding facility. From there, he managed to get himself to a distant state where his family of origin resided.

In 2001, David became a priest of the Catholic Charismatic Church, later with the Holy Catholic Church International. He now serves hospitals and nursing homes as a volunteer chaplain plus he continues a ministry of counseling.

At this writing, he is almost 69 years old, as am I. He has discovered his own soul as a priest and Christian clinical counselor, firmly convinced that his suffering had very great value: enabling the empathy necessary for being a truly effective therapist. The results with his patients through the years have bordered on the miraculous.

He also realizes that his cross, which he still carries, is the very proof that he is loved by his Savior. He takes up his cross daily and follows with joyful fulfillment, hope, and excitement.

11 Child Abuse Treatment

When I first moved to Jacksonville, Florida, from Philadelphia in 1985, one of the first things I did was to purchase a boat. Unfortunately, I chose a second-hand model without knowing anything about how to fix it. Every time it broke down, and that seemed to be at least once a week, I needed to head straight to the parts department of the local marina store and buy another part that I hoped would make the engine run again. In time, I had spent more on parts than I had for the boat itself. When a friend found out what I had been doing, he said, "You can't do that. You have to find the problem and fix it."

The same principle needs to be applied in treating children who have been abused. Just as schools affix meaningless labels to children with learning or behavioral difficulties, many who attempt to treat children follow an inflexible model. A big part of the problem is that not enough is known about the impact of child abuse on the individual. Every "self" is different from every other. Even identical twins are far apart in the way they interpret and react to the very same life experiences.

Therefore, "child abuse" is no more a diagnosis than is "fever" for pneumonia or "anoxia" for a specific cognitive impairment. Every treatment plan must begin with an accurate diagnosis, not in the form of a label, but instead encompassing the major life factors the child has dealt with and will or could face in the future, all in light of his present suffering.

The few adequate outcome studies on treatment reveal a miserable level of success, and it is my contention that the failure rate is due to the treatment methodologies being both over-standardized and based on too little information about what child abuse does to the individual child, in addition to general, categorized, diagnoses and lack of focus in treatment. After the review of 20 years' worth of studies, encompassing hundreds of thousands of sexually abused children, there is little evidence to support the belief that therapy facilitates recovery (Finkelhor and Berliner, 1995).

One of the largest obstacles to effective treatment, in my view, is that children do not fit well into medical-model diagnostic categories. By and large, children do not suffer from "mental illness" but instead react to the conditions of their lives. They form adjustments or maladjustments to reality. In order to help a child, it is necessary to pinpoint and do something about the life factors that are causing him to suffer, underperform, or misbehave.

If the diagnosis is both accurate and comprehensive, and the treatment is focused not on theory but on reality, then the child will respond, provided that the therapist knows how to treat abused children. It must always be remembered that there is no normal way to react to craziness. There will be a reaction of some kind, in the form of symptoms. These symptoms erroneously form the basis for the present method of diagnosis.

Most therapists, whether psychiatrists, psychologists, social workers, or mental-health counselors, have no idea how to treat abused children, because the subject is not taught in their graduate curriculum. The most prevailing mental-health issue of our time has not found its way to the graduate-school classroom. Any information so far developed has been gathered through individual research studies, which must be "hunted down" by any professional interested in the subject.

Such organizations as the American Professional Society on the Abuse of Children (APSAC) and the International Society for Traumatic Stress Studies (ISTSS), to name my two favorites, should be joined by every professional in the field, including attorneys. Their journals should be standard reading.

Another factor sabotaging outcome results is that "therapy" has no endpoint but instead continues on until the process becomes destructive rather than helpful. Prolonged, weekly encounters with the therapist can keep the original trauma alive, cause over-dependency on the therapist, and re-convince the child that there is something wrong with him, the very mindset that he came in with. The major goal is for the child to understand at the deepest level that the problem is outside of him. He is not the problem. The problem is that he has had to suffer needlessly, and a way must be found to improve his life circumstances. If these life circumstances are not changed, the child will continue to react.

Again, in any therapy for any condition, it must always be remembered that there is no normal way to react to craziness in any form. Nor is there any normal way to react to maltreatment or neglect.

Therefore, the very first factor in forming a diagnosis and treatment plan is to find out what the child is reacting to, and this evaluation demands a thorough study of home life and the histories of the caregivers.

Next, the child must be set free from all blame. It cannot be emphasized strongly enough that the child believes that the maltreatment is his fault. Following that accomplishment, treating either trauma or information deficiencies will be necessary.

In the treatment of trauma, the damaging events must be brought to full consciousness, and then they must be recast in order to make sense for processing. Obviously, the establishment of a feeling of complete safety and trust is required, and for this reason, actual therapy may not begin immediately. Instead, the child should be allowed to play at something he truly enjoys, be it a video game, a board game with the therapist being a player, or whatever. Nothing can be accomplished until the child feels safe with the therapist. In this regard, I urge every therapist to study carefully the book *Gentling: A Practical Guide to Treating PTSD in Abused Children 2nd Ed.* by William Krill.

This consideration brings up the matter of whether the therapist should be male or female, especially in cases where the child is female and the abuser is male. Ideally, since the harm was inflicted by a male, a more complete processing can be accomplished when the therapist is also male. Many times, however, this is not possible because the child is too upset. The factor must still be considered in the case of little boys; but with female children, the importance is greater.

When the child has reached a level of comfort and safety, and he trusts the therapist, there is a technique that can be used to bring the traumatic events to the present with minimal upset. The child can be given a toy telescope to focus on a completely blank wall. As he is complying, suggestions of progressive relaxation can be given to bring the child to a relaxed state and heightened suggestibility. Full-scale hypnosis is not recommended because in rare instances, the child can become overwhelmingly upset when his defenses are down. Also, hypnotic recall does not hold up well in court.

[Contrary to popular belief, it is not necessary for the child to remember the details of his traumatic event or events. An understanding of the general nature of his wounding is all that is required, to be followed by insight into how the trauma has impacted his life, most importantly, his view of himself.]

Next, it can be suggested that he is in his favorite place, where he feels safest of all, and where he is happy. He can be told that he is now looking at a movie of himself, but that he is still in the safe place. Now he can be asked about the bad parts of the movie. The child may go very far the first time, or he may not be able to comply at all, in which case the procedure is repeated later. He is informed that being able to play this "game" is a goal that will continue to be worked on. He should be praised for his hard work, no matter how little he has accomplished.

When the child has been able to describe the traumatic events, the time has arrived for a thorough discussion of them, with the emphasis on making sense for processing. Some meaning and explanation must be attached to these recollections so that the child can move past them. One form of talking about the trauma is the recommended interview for a forensic evaluation, as shown below. Known as the "cognitive interview", it is also very useful for court testimony when required (Walker, 1994).

> First, have the child reconstruct the circumstances of the crime by encouraging her to put herself in the place and time that the abuse occurred—e.g., "picture it as if you are there right now." To ensure the child focuses on actual events, do not use words "imagine", "pretend", or "story". Second, report everything the child says. Ask her to tell you as much information as possible, even seemingly unimportant details. After the child finishes her narrative description, follow with questions to clarify what was said. Third, go through the incident from the beginning to the end, then reverse the order and go through it again. Finally, encourage the child to recount events from different perspectives—e.g., "if you were sitting in the corner of the room, what would you have seen?"

Again, the above procedure is to be performed only after the child has mastered the telescope task. This process of the child's recounting the abuse from different perspectives and repeating the account more than once not only opens possibilities for explanatory discussion but also tends to desensitize the child's internal responses.

Next, the child can be assisted in writing a letter to the abuser, without holding back any words of emotional expression. The child is assured that whether the letter is mailed or not will be decided later, and the decision will be his alone.

When neglect rather than direct abuse is at issue, the therapist should engage the child in play and praise the child for everything done—or at least comment on every activity. Ongoing interaction with positive regard is the thrust. A goal is for the child to be convinced that an important adult truly cares about him and is interested in what he says and does.

Beyond this goal, it is necessary to work with educators and social workers to ensure placement in a stimulating milieu where praise, appropriate affection, and plentiful attention will be guaranteed. In most cases, if the child is placed in a foster home, it will be better if the child is the only one in care, at least for several months.

If the "Inventory for Concealed Child Abuse" has been used prior to therapy, it can again be given for comparison. A significant reduction in the number of positive responses could help form a possible measure of outcome.

One further thought here is that almost any form of child treatment demands a team approach. Social services agencies, educators, school counselors, pediatricians, and perhaps child-advocacy attorneys are some of the resources that must be relied on heavily. In this regard, it is absolutely essential that these people have a firm understanding of what the child's needs are, what the therapist is trying to accomplish, and why. Also, it should be cautioned that if court testimony is required, the therapist must speak in plain English, in an open and relaxed manner, with "psycho-babble" avoided at all costs.

Regarding court testimony, it is often the practice of an attorney to force an expert witness to answer a question with only a "yes" or "no". In that case, I turn to the judge and say, "Your Honor, I have sworn to tell the whole truth, and I cannot with a simple "yes" or "no". This technique has allowed me to be far more effective in my testimony.

12 | **Treatment of Adult Survivors**

Most of the domestic-abuse survivors I have worked with have a history of multiple abusive ("romantic") relationships beginning in adolescence and continuing into adulthood. When there is an exception, the survivor has found a man of endless patience who is willing to endure the extremely trying behavior that resembles a borderline personality disorder. This is the case because most are suffering from post-traumatic stress disorder (PTSD) or a symptomatic picture closely resembling it.

Judith Herman (1992) boldly exposes the rampant misdiagnoses of trauma victims and calls the overlooked diagnosis of posttraumatic stress disorder an epidemic. To be discussed shortly, the diagnosis of borderline personality disorder is one of the most insulting that any doctor could pick from the list of diagnostic criteria.

My male patients tend to fall into one of several descriptive categories: hostility toward women in general due to abuse by their mothers; past criminal activity, always associated with alcohol or drugs; PTSD; or any combination of the above. With few exceptions, the men are of above-average to high intelligence, but working in low-level jobs and are completely blinded as to their true selves and potential. Occasionally, a man will present with a previous history of either schizophrenia or bi-polar psychotic illness, and their symptoms, if considered in isolation, somewhat justify such a misdiagnosis.

Regardless of gender, prior misdiagnoses are most often found in patients with the most severe childhood trauma, combined with the least recall of what happened.

According to Dr. Herman, who received the Guttmacher Award by the American Psychiatric Association, abuse victims are falling through the cracks when it comes to correct diagnosis and treatment. She propounds that up to 60 percent of psychiatric patients, both inpatient and outpatient, report childhood histories of physical or sexual abuse or both. This estimate excludes emotional abuse and neglect. She believes, and my experience confirms, that these patients are suffering from PTSD as a direct result of childhood maltreatment.

Some psychologists and psychiatrists know what to expect in the way of symptomatology with war veterans: PTSD. We know as a fact that, even in the strongest individual, the experiences of war can produce the constellation of symptoms that therapists should recognize as trauma. But for some reason, we have only begun to make this same connection with people whose lives have been a "war".

One woman, Catherine, spent nearly 20 years in therapy, first with an educational counselor, then three psychiatrists, one by one, plus a family therapist. She found herself with suicidal feelings right up to the time she entered our group for domestic abuse. One psychiatrist, an analyst, spent two years asking her, "What do you think?" Another psychiatrist gave her open prescriptions for highly addictive drugs, and the third psychiatrist wanted to use electroconvulsive therapy, probably the worst possible treatment for trauma survivors. The family therapist ordered her to draw a family genealogy chart.

None of the above professionals seemed determined to find the cause of her suffering; they just had their favorite ways of treating symptoms. Catherine's real problem had been nightly incest at the hands of her biological father, the rejection by her mother as a result, and constant debasing comments by both parents and both sisters all of her life. Not even her head-banging, a dead giveaway for sexual abuse, was noticed.

Another woman, Lynn, was in treatment for 30 years for depression and "borderline personality disorder", 10 of these years with the same psychiatrist. When the decade had passed, he remarked, "I really don't think I can help you." Never was Lynne's sadistically violent tormentor, her husband, ever asked about or seen.

None of her therapists had been interested in causality. A disinterest in root cause is, in my opinion, the greatest weakness in the mental health professions. We have clung so closely to the medical model that emotional disturbances of almost any kind have historically been seen as free-standing, as though they had arisen from an infection, from a vacuum, or from nowhere. How this mentality has survived is a mystery, when in any other science, the principle of cause and effect rules.

Put another way, for every action there is a reaction. Molest, torture, humiliate, or neglect a child severely enough, and PTSD or similar symptoms will be the reaction. For this reason, the treatment of domestic abuse is the treatment of child abuse, and both are the treatment of trauma. Here are some of the diagnostic indicators of PTSD (American Psychiatric Association, 1994):

- The patient has experienced a life-threatening or unspeakable event involving self or someone close, or has lived through a horrible period in life.
- The response consisted of fear, helplessness, or horror.
- The event(s) is re-experienced even though it may have occurred long ago; for example:
  - Memories, images, flashbacks
  - Nightmares
  - Feeling as though the event is happening now
  - Numbing or freezing of emotions
  - Dissociation
  - Intense distress triggered by reminders.
- Avoidance behavior is exhibited; for example:
  - Avoiding thoughts, feelings, conversations regarding the event(s)
  - Avoiding people, places, things that trigger emotion.
- Inability to recall an important part of the event.
- Diminished interest in normal activities.
- Feeling detached from others.
- Restricted range of emotions or episodic rage.
- Sense of foreshortened future.
- Hyperarousal, including:
  - Difficulty falling or staying asleep.
  - Irritability.
  - Difficulty concentrating.
  - Hypervigilance.
  - Exaggerated startle response.
- Depersonalization.
- Derealization.

Notice the reference to an "inability to recall an important part of the event". Despite all the controversy, repressed memories are an actuality found frequently in abuse survivors. This phenomenon, I believe, can be explained cognitively if one considers two things: 1) a child cannot process an event that makes no sense or that is too overwhelming for his interpretation; and 2) dissociation, a natural defense common to all children, blocks out most of the memory so that any recall will be weak at best.

There is a way to determine whether a memory is valid or not. If the recall of a terrifying or unspeakable event is valid, the result will usually be relief rather than further terror, provided that the recall occurs in a supportive environment after safety has been well-established. Conversely, "false memories", or those instigated by the therapist, will usually upset the patient even more. This is not to say that accurate recall will, of itself, be curative, but it will bring great comfort and encouragement even though cognitive processing, desensitization, and other measures must follow successfully. Recall brings relief because it brings with it an explanation of what had seemed to be symptoms of mental illness. Most importantly, recall establishes who really is the problem.

Without exception, every patient I have ever treated for anything, all through my 28 years of practice, has had a basis in reality for the symptoms, as serious as they may have been.

Sometimes part of the reality lies in genetic predisposition, such as with alcoholism, schizophrenia, and bi-polar illness. Often there are strong biochemical factors that must be dealt with pharmacologically. But these biologic factors, as important as they are, do not explain everything.

Why, for example, have the schizophrenics I've treated been raised either in chaos or in an environment where there has been no communication? How does one learn to think when no one has taught him? What else can the child use as a navigation system besides his feelings, with his emotions being his only guide in how to react? Also, if put under enough stress, everyone will break. The nature of the resulting pattern depends on genetic weaknesses, which all of us have, but they vary among people. So, if the family situation is bad, one person may end up schizophrenic, another depressed, etc.

As a further example, and the most important for the purposes of this book, let us look at the criteria for borderline personality disorder (American Psychiatric Association, 1994) in light of child abuse and resultant trauma. (APA criteria are indented, and my comments appear in plain text.)

Borderline Personality Disorder

- A pervasive pattern of instability of interpersonal relationships, self-image and affects, and marked impulsivity beginning by early adulthood and present in a variety of contexts, as indicated by five (or more) of the following:

- Frantic efforts to avoid real or imagined abandonment. Note: Do not include suicidal or self-mutilating behavior covered in criterion 5.

An abused child has been denied the full exploration of the true self, as well as imaginary becoming and the taste of power. A neglected child has been abandoned repeatedly in real life.

- A pattern of unstable and intense interpersonal relationships characterized by alternating between extremes of idealization and devaluation.

The abused child's first relationships were the cause of shame, debasement, pain, and terror. The trust-versus-mistrust developmental process has been sabotaged. Abused children typically end up in a series of abusive relationships in late adolescence and both early and late adulthood.

- Identity disturbance: markedly and persistently unstable self-image or sense of self.

Child abuse and neglect eradicate personhood and cause the formation of a false self that operates either on the illusion of power or the illusion of powerlessness. The true self is covered up beyond recognition.

- Impulsivity in at least two areas that are potentially self-damaging (e.g., spending, sex, substance abuse, reckless driving, binge eating). Note: Do not include suicidal or self-mutilating behavior covered in Criterion 5.

Besides the problem-solving goal in sexually acting out, sex is a cheap substitute, or "quick fix", for the love a deluded person thinks is impossible to acquire. Substance abuse occurs in the majority of cases involving incest. Both binge eating and spending are, as patients themselves report, an effort to fill the emptiness they feel inside.

- Recurrent suicidal behavior, gestures, or threats, or self-mutilating behavior.

Patients traumatized by severe child abuse report sudden suicidal urges and compulsions to harm themselves (especially symbolic, surface cutting of the wrist area) when they are overcome with the original message of being bad. The suppressed rage that naturally occurs as a result of the atrocities they have suffered will, at times when it breaks through the mental restraints, be aimed at self as a type of "substitute murder" whereby one's own self is killed rather than the abuser.

- Affective instability due to a marked reactivity of mood (e.g., intense episodic dysphoria, irritability, or anxiety usually lasting a few hours and only rarely more than a few days).

These are "flashback" reactions triggered by reminders of the original abuse. The surge of feelings resembles one's listening to an old song on the radio whereby the exact emotional tone of the time returns completely. The mood reaction dissipates when the flashback is no longer fresh in the mind.

- Chronic feelings of emptiness.

My traumatized patients report always feeling empty, with the emptiness most acute at times when they feel completely out of touch with any sense of being. Depersonalization, a consequence of abuse, leads to derealization, including the feeling of being empty inside-as though "no one is home."

Many, many celebrities have this terrifying problem and therefore end up using alcohol or drugs as self-medication and eventually over-using to the point of life-threatening addiction. Hence, the frequent incidence of alcohol and other drug abuse among them. A great number enter the entertainment professions in order to be affirmed as "people", to find an identity that they would not otherwise have.

- Inappropriate, intense anger or difficulty controlling anger (e.g., frequent displays of temper, constant anger, recurrent physical fights).

Not only anger, but also rage, is the primary symptom of trauma. While male survivors tend to be direct and aggressive at times, women are more typically passive, with their anger being expressed through manipulation or complaining, sometimes alternating with depression.

- Transient, stress-related paranoid ideation or severe dissociative symptoms.

Hypervigilance, severe enough to appear paranoid, is a primary symptom of trauma. And no wonder, since these victims have been betrayed, hurt, insulted, debased, and mangled without warning their entire lives. Dissociation occurs often during the time of the original abuse due to the fact that the child does not have the mental resources to comprehend the horrors that are being inflicted. The child finds that "going away" mentally is an effective way to deal with terror, and the practice continues into adulthood.

Thus it can be seen that this so-called personality disorder can be, at least in many cases, a reaction to the utterly absurd or unbearable.

Mental Illness as Reaction to Craziness

Seeing not just the above criteria but those of other personality disorders in this light raises a very provocative question: Are many forms of mental illness a reaction? Not putting aside biological and chemical factors, does this "reaction" concept fill in some voids in beginning to understand this unwieldy, mysterious, ill-defined matter we call "mental illness?"

If a child is raised in an abusive or neglectful environment, could anyone put together a reasonable description of what a normal response would be? Is there a normal way to respond to the preposterous or to outright craziness? Is there a "correct" way to adapt to what M. Scott Peck terms "evil"?

Trauma symptoms, as Herman courageously puts forth, are the end result of child abuse. Place a strong and brave soldier in combat that is terrifying enough, horrifying enough, painful enough, intense enough, and long enough, and a "classic" trauma picture will emerge. Is this hero mentally ill?

The Indestructible Soul

One beginning principle that helps give adult survivors of child abuse and domestic abuse hope in their early treatment is the indestructibility of the "self", or soul. My treatment regimen strongly encourages spirituality. Belief in the loving, all-powerful God of Christians and Jews facilitates the overcoming of powerlessness and rejection. I go so far as to insist that the self and the mind are in all reality one entity: the eternal soul. Seen from this point of view, the self can be mangled but not destroyed.

The soul can be fooled, betrayed, injured, abandoned, and tortured beyond endurance; but it cannot be killed. No matter how thoroughly bashed a soul has been, it can be revived when the lies of abuse are systematically removed… when the false messages are dissected one by one and replaced with valid discoveries about one's true self—the soul.

Sense of Purpose Absolutely Required

The most important and lasting gifts that parents can give their children have nothing to do with material things. For example, a top priority for parents is to give the child, in the teen years, a sense of purpose; that is, to encourage him to discover his (or her) calling in the Kingdom of God.

The sad fact is that most people go to their graves without ever knowing why they were born in the first place. The popular way to find one's niche in life is by trial and error, but rarely does this method work. Herein lies the chief reason that so many adults are miserable in their jobs.

Teach your child that the only way to find his calling is to ask, in prayer. And one must ask and ask until an answer is given. Persistence is essential.

But how does God answer? I have found two ways, but there must be many others. One way is that the Lord will increase an existing desire of the heart toward one pursuit, and another is that He may instill a brand new one that seems to come from nowhere. He has used both of these for me.

Perhaps this introduction justifies a discussion of us all; that is, how do we find out what we are supposed to do in this life? It is never too late to obtain an answer.

Sometimes we are given an initial purpose that may change. In other words, our calling may be for a season only and therefore destined to be replaced by another at some point. In my case, I have been a broadcaster, an editor, a publicist, the vice-president of a prominent marketing company, a family therapist, a licensed psychologist, and a priest. The last one is my final assignment, I am sure.

I am also certain that the earlier assignments did prepare me for my present role. So if you are advanced in years and wonder if there could be any options left, the answer is "yes".

Also, our calling may be the way we make our living, or it may be completely unrelated. I have known powerfully gifted people whose dynamic and productive ministries have had nothing to do with generating income.

The most important thing to remember is that God has created all of us as unique individuals with a life-path unlike anyone else's. Above all, we must pursue His will for our lives, because His way is the only one that provides for maximum fulfillment and joy.

Some of the mistakes we make in this journey are by accepting what our parents think we should be, by pursuing the profession or occupation of a parent, by either over-valuing our abilities or under-valuing them, and by doing what we guess would be fun.

It may well be that we are destined to follow the occupational path of a parent, or that assumption might be absolutely wrong—even tragically mistaken. Any idea we have in this regard must be presented to God. We cannot guess or even follow what we are convinced is correct. The only safe way is to follow directions.

Years ago, my son-in-law gave me Rick Warren's *Purpose-Driven Life* (2002). My reaction to reading it was that I thought these principles were so basic that everybody knew them. Since that time, I have discovered that few people understand Reverend Warren's principles. His book has been an inspiration to millions. I wish I could have written it myself more than 40 years ago.

Recalling Traumatic Events

For years now, I have been using a method of treating abused people by expanding on some principles I learned from Dr. Louis Tinnin, Professor Emeritus at the University of West Virginia. A therapist rather naturally develops his own style after many imitations of a good method.

Most of my patients have been women who were abused in a frightening way during childhood. Many of them know that something bad happened, and they are haunted, but they are not sure why. They cannot in most cases remember the incident, at least not all of it.

My method helps recover repressed memories. My patients for the most part are convinced that there is something to recall. Therefore, I am not implanting any false memory.

First, I ask the patient to think diligently about a place they have encountered in life that has given them the greatest sense of complete safety and happiness. Then I have her (or him) discuss that place at some length, in order to refresh the experience of peace. When she has a firm hold on that location, I move to the next step.

I lead her through the standard process of progressive relaxation and stop just short of a somnambulistic state. At most, she is in a light trance. Then it is explained that she is now in her safe place and will stay there until I ask her to come back. Staying in the safe place is emphasized repeatedly.

Next, I suggest to her that she is looking through a magic telescope and that she can look at anything at any stage in her life without the slightest upset because she is far away in her safety zone, where she remains at peace no matter what. Anything that would even seem scary or sad will only make her happier to be where she is.

I ask her never to stop looking through the magic telescope and never to leave her safe place. Then I ask her to focus in on various stages of her life, especially early childhood, and tell me if she sees anything unpleasant. If so, I remind her that she is merely looking through a magic telescope from far, far, away.

Those with true repressed or incompletely formed memories quickly come to the traumatic incident. More reassurance is piled on at that time. Then she is asked whether or not she would like to describe what she sees. Usually she does want to share, but she is given the choice to postpone any description until a later time if she so wishes.

Again, most patients exhibit relief at the discovery and want to talk about it at length. Many are elated that they can look right at the ugliness with vivid recall and yet not be upset. They feel unburdened and set free. During any discussion, they remain in the safe place.

After the event has been described thoroughly, I bring them back to their normal state, back to reality. I point out that monsters have power only in the dark, and that now there is bright light. Further talk therapy follows, either during the same session or at the next one. The decision is left completely to the patient.

Before leaving, she is given a telephone number by which she can reach me at any time that she feels that she may become upset. She is urged to call at the first sign of upset.

It must be strongly emphasized that the procedure must be stopped immediately at any point when there is a sign of upset; if not stopped, at least paused until the patient is ready to proceed. Sometimes patients are reluctant to go through the procedure, and that fact must be honored.

There are also many patients who remember too well what happened to them and thus cannot discuss the trauma. I have found that a similar procedure is effective in these cases as well.

When the above is followed up by same-sex group therapy, strong supportive bonds form quickly. The participants in the groups focus on empowerment, the process of becoming, the discovery of the true self that has been covered up most of their lives. They come to understand that abuse has altered their concept of self and given them a false identity laden with guilt and a second-class mentality.

Reliance on the Holy Spirit

It is beautiful and most rewarding to watch this process of unfolding during these group sessions. I have seen women go from a position of perceived helplessness to one of great confidence and productivity.

My co-therapist for several years was a psychiatric nurse who had enjoyed a successful career before being brutalized by her husband. She began as my patient and became my co-therapist. She went on to represent herself in court proceedings against her ex-husband, who was a federal district judge.

I have long believed that no psychotherapist can facilitate real change without a supernatural anointing. In other words, counseling and psychotherapy require a gifting through the Holy Spirit.

This premise applies in a powerful way to victims of child and domestic abuse. Only a survivor of such prolonged and intense suffering can understand what another is experiencing. I mean flashbacks, fragmented memories that force their way into consciousness, nightmares, depression, rage, and all else that are consequences of having your whole personality mangled by abuse.

Dangers of False Spirituality

I have had complete strangers walk up to me and ask in a confrontational way, "Do you know Jesus Christ as your personal Lord and Savior?" As if they didn't notice the collar I was wearing, I have responded, "Of course I do!"

It was not through some emotion-charged experience that I have come to know Christ but rather through the sufferings that he has allowed me to bear and from which he has delivered me. He has brought me through extreme suffering time and again, and each time I have felt his presence more profoundly.

I am tempted to answer these new and giddy Christians with the request, "Show me your cross." The measure of mature Christian faith is the weight of our cross and how well we bear it. Jesus firmly taught that if we are to come after him, we must deny ourselves, take up our cross, and follow him.

He meant that we must keep on going no matter how heavy our cross is. But we find that the longer we follow him, the lighter our cross becomes. We learn that our own suffering is nothing compared to what he suffered for us. Further, the longer we travel with him faithfully, the more bearable our cross becomes. We reach the understanding that it is precisely our suffering that joins us to him.

It is at this point that our joy becomes more complete because the cross confirms that we belong to him, that we have in fact been adopted. We have become residents of the heavenly kingdom where we shall live eternally without any cross of any kind.

Jesus said that those who suffer are blessed because they shall be comforted. This comfort goes beyond relief in our present trial but extends to lasting peace. The next time we are challenged, we can face the circumstances with much less fear because we have learned that the Comforter, the Holy Spirit, is about to arrive.

In addition, we gain empathy combined with an increased capacity to love others. Jesus said that the world would know we belong to him by the way we love one another. I have never seen much love or compassion in a so-called Christian who has led a trouble-free life.

I remember the man who came to me for counseling. He had practiced successfully the heretical "prosperity doctrine" and had acquired a very high-end lifestyle. Yet he was empty and in fact agitated. He moaned that when people see the two luxury cars in the driveway and the size of his house, they do not consider what it takes to keep these things.

His possessions had come to own him instead of the other way around. Had he followed the suggestion of Jesus and sold all he had and given it to the poor, he would have received comfort.

Dealing with Impossible People

Learning to relate to difficult people is one of the most common and anguishing problems I've encountered in many years as a Christian psychotherapist and psychologist.

Toxic relationships between two parties seem to endure as long as healthy ones, and sometimes longer, for they tend to be permanent. The difficult party holds more power than the other, who is forever trying to please or get the approval of the dominator.

The dominator remains inflexible in rejecting very imaginative attempts by the subjective party to achieve victory. But no success is ever possible. No matter what the words or actions of the would-be pleaser, the unpleased remains unmoved and continues to insult and otherwise depersonalize the one in the weaker position.

We all have seen these destructive arrangements between husbands and wives, siblings, close friends, and other social connections, including the workplace. Whether at work or at home, negative forces such as these tend to enslave.

The power holder maintains position throughout time, and the underling obeys the rules of the relationship as well. Even though the unspoken agreement between the parties is absurd, it is honored nonetheless.

Oddly, the subservience of the underdog fosters quite admirable achievements. Therefore, it is not usual for the pleaser to attain a higher social or professional rank than the one who will never be appeased.

I have seen this regrettable dynamic at play most often between mother and daughter, with competition between siblings running a close second.

One of the worst examples is the proverbial mother whose daughter is never permitted to please her. The mother communicates without words that "it's your job to make me happy," but nothing you ever do will work. Some of these daughters develop anorexia as a result of feeling as an absolute failure in their only mission in life.

Even though there seems to be no solution, there really is.

One of the parties must break a major rule governing the contract. In other words, somebody needs to start acting and reacting in ways that the other would never predict.

By far the most effective response is for one of the parties to refuse a cue and not respond at all. The initiator, never having faced such a surprise, has no way to come back. Further, the dominator is foiled in the insane game's objective to wound the other. The pay-off is denied.

In the movie "War Games", a hit many years ago, a computer in the War Room of the Department of Defense is put through an accelerated exercise to predict the outcome of various military strikes with the probable retaliatory action by the enemy and vice-versa.

The enlarged computer screen becomes a flashing light, a rapid strobe, as the computer rushes through every possible scenario. Finally, the screen freezes with the words: "The only solution is not to play."

Therapist Qualifications

Wounded healers are by far the most effective psychotherapists. This belief persists so strongly in me that, as president of a seminary training Christian counselors, I count the student's own suffering as the most important element by far in his or her education.

What I am about to say will seem preposterous to traditional educators. I purposely seek victims and survivors of abuse as students. Then I counsel them by telephone at the same time that I am acting as their curriculum advisor.

They receive both education and therapy by phone when they are enrolled and actively pursuing their demanding studies.

One particular young woman, who calls me several times a week long-distance, has the worst history of abuse I have ever heard of in nearly 30 years as a therapist in this field. She is being educated and healed at the same time.

When this lady is fully empowered by this process, and when her doctoral requirements are met, she will be a Christian therapist with the insight and wisdom that only suffering could achieve. God will take every bit of her terror, physical pain, shame, and self-doubt and transform the package into a priceless gift for healing others.

The question of why bad things happen to good people still circulates among us, but there is at least one real answer—that our suffering can lead to dynamic service in the Kingdom of God.

One key is to change our point of view about ourselves from that of victim to that of survivor. Such a re-framing changes everything. We come to see that there was meaning and purpose all along in what we endured. Our trials were not for nothing. They were the foundation for a life of service.

This premise holds true for many other kinds of victims having the symptoms of trauma. I have learned that all victims of physical or sexual abuse exhibit signs of trauma. Since abuse survivors share this condition with so many people, they can be a resource that is in very great demand.

Therapists able to treat any kind of trauma are extremely rare. For example, war veterans typically have a prolonged wait for treatment simply because specialists in this field are in such short supply.

We have abuse as a growing pandemic; we have war veterans; and we have millions of more people who have been traumatized by some event. The shortage of help is disastrous. The best place to look for potential therapists is in the population of victims becoming survivors.

I have been a Christian counselor for more than 28 years, and I was also a licensed psychologist at one time. There were many outcomes in therapy that I consider miraculous recoveries.

The trouble was, however, that this work exhausted me. The reason is that I tried too hard. Instead of relying on the power of God, whom I believe had appointed me, I depended too much on my own efforts. When I look back now, I can see plainly that the most dramatic results occurred without my doing, and that I was only a witness.

Self-Confidence, a Hazard

I have a message for those who feel called to some ministry: Do not be afraid. You do not have to trust in yourself. In fact, self-confidence will block you as a channel of heavenly power and love. Rely on God alone, and pray for a huge increase in faith. Remember, He does not choose people who are capable: He endows those who are willing.

I think God wants His servants to get busy, for time is short. His intention is to make full use of our gifts during our lifetimes and to prevent them from being dormant, as many are. There is much, much work to be done.

Remember that the purpose of serving others is not only to relieve suffering but more importantly to lead the afflicted to their Maker. If you are a genuine servant, then you know that you are blessed greatly whenever you, under His power, bless another. During such times, you sense the Lord's reality in a rare and most holy way.

I think all believers, Jews and Christians, are gifted in some way. But most have no idea of what has been pre-ordained for them to do. They cannot find out through trial and error: they must ask; they must ask and ask until they know they have the answer.

Then they must prepare themselves by acquiring the knowledge needed, while at the same time seeking a closer relationship with God through prayer and meditation as well as by immersing themselves in all that is beautiful and true.

While earthly knowledge is very limited, learning remains a great virtue. "Study to show thyself approved," as the Holy Scriptures command. Do not go forth in ignorance to try to serve. In the case of preaching, for example, there are men and women everywhere who know very well what the Bible says. But they have no idea what the scriptures mean.

They are not educated in the history of the Church nor in the teachings put forth throughout history by true saints. I mean by "saint" not just anyone who has been saved but only one who has lived a life of heroic virtue and through whom miracles have been performed, even after the saint's death.

Jesus did not come to Earth to become a famous author and then to go away and leave us only with a book, as holy as it is. His intention was to establish a living, breathing Church with the authority to teach the truth. He has spoken through His chosen ones throughout the ages, and especially during the very worst of times.

He continues to guide His people, and He always will. But not everyone who proclaims himself to be a preacher, pastor, prophet, or healer is truly appointed, called by God. Most are not.

In Jacksonville, Florida, where I live, there are over 3,000 churches, most of them independent, and preaching whatever the so-called pastor fancies. In most cases, their education is sorely lacking. Those with the least knowledge but the loudest music seem to grow the fastest. This trend seems to hold true throughout the United States. These matters are discussed more fully in the chapter on special populations.

I had a close friend years ago whose pastor was a former exterminator. My friend had a phobia of roaches. When he yelled one time after seeing one in his kitchen, I told him to call his pastor.

My point is that we must rely on God's power when we minister to another, but we also need to be prepared educationally and never stop being a student.

13 | A New 7-Step Program

Advantages of Group Therapy

When the early communications that still live in the brain are put on trial, and the credentials of those "experts" who implanted the ideas are challenged by a group, the roots of delusion are loosened and eventually pulled. Then there remains fertile soil in which to plant the truth: the indisputable facts of one's own successes and talents never before considered are explored and brought to life.

Similarly, the process of discovering one's true self is facilitated by the examination of one's values. I can think of no other factor that more describes the true self than one's value system. Typically, as one powerful exercise, I take out a sheet of paper and write down the traits that the patient admires in other people, be they celebrities or people they have come to learn about or know well during their lives. When the list is complete, I hand it back to the patient and instruct her to write her own name at the top. Then I ask her to affix it to her refrigerator or bedroom mirror and add to it daily, every time she thinks of something else.

Many a patient has held another person in awe due to some very positive characteristics of a personal or characterological, nature. Those qualities admired in another person are already one's own. Such is self-evident. How could another's attributes be valued unless the value itself is part of one's own true nature? All patients see the point very clearly.

Patients are uniformly buoyed by the realization that there is an understandable explanation for why they are in their present state of suffering—that their condition does not have to remain shrouded in mystery, and especially that they are not hopelessly mentally ill or otherwise inferior to other people. I tell every patient I see that we'll together come to know the cause of the distress and then go to work to "fix" it. The adage "Knowing the problem is half the solution" is gloriously true in psychotherapy, no matter what the presenting condition.

Critical Importance of Safety

Effective treatment cannot proceed until the patient is first comfortable with the therapist and then comfortable in the therapy group. In the group, which I have found to be the most effective method, as have many others, there must be certain ground rules. Importantly, no one is ever encouraged to speak about herself until she really wants to share. No group member may criticize or insult another. All members must give a genuinely warm welcome to newcomers (and they do, from the heart). Each member must commit to attendance each time (once a week for 90 minutes, with a break after 45 minutes).

Also, the group must be small, preferably not more than 10. After that number, a new group is begun. It is vital that the group be stabilized so that all members know each other well and have no fear of another member. They are encouraged to exchange phone numbers and use them often in order to establish an enduring emotional resource.

Typically, the group becomes so cohesive that they plan social events together in addition to going out to eat after the sessions. They visit each other when sick, and call an absent member to make sure she is all right. All of this is done out of genuine concern for each other. In other words, they become closer than sisters.

A newcomer will usually remain silent for a session or two before she begins to share. But when the time comes, she experiences an immediate partial healing because for the first time in her life, she is able to have her feelings and her prior behavior understood and validated. All of her life, she has been told to minimize her trauma and "just get over it." However, this has always been impossible because the events of her life have made no sense and therefore could not be processed. Besides that, similar events keep happening, over and over.

When she finds a group of women who have suffered in very similar ways, and they say, "I understand, and I feel what you feel," her life-long search to connect with another person has finally succeeded. She feels as though she has been touched and made into a person entitled to her feelings, reactions, and behaviors.

Usually, a patient will address one or members of the group when she is talking, rather than the therapist. The therapist, however, directs the course of the discussion and frequently intercedes with insights or explanations. He acts as a protector for all members and jumps in at the slightest hint of anything threatening to anyone. When the conversation becomes too intense, he switches to a lighter subject and then later returns to the difficult matter.

When the group is first initiated, the therapist spends several sessions explaining what trauma is and how it is the natural result of abuse. He further shows that child abuse typically leads to abusive relationships in later life. The therapist is accompanied by a female co-facilitator, in our case an experienced psychiatric nurse who is very motherly.

As the group addresses actual experiences of the members, the sessions are alternated so that after a session of intense sharing, the next session is devoted to a lighter subject.

Each session brings reports of new power acquisition in their interpersonal affairs; that is, examples of self-assertion or simply doing something kind for one's self. Since abuse results in powerlessness, the acquisition of power on many fronts helps propel the course of therapy and provides the courage to examine the past.

There must come a time of life when a person turns around and takes a look back to ask the question, "Were my parents correct about me? Did they give me the truth about who I really am, or did they give me messages distorted by who they were?" We must be adventurous, full of courage, in order to decide what information to keep and what to throw out. We must find out who we are in fact.

Those who are spiritual-minded begin by finding out *why* they are, and this discovery tends to lead to *who* they are. Many come to believe that a life plan has been prearranged for them by their supreme being, and that they have a special place in this world. All are therefore encouraged constantly to explore any hidden talents or abilities that they may have thought about as small children sitting on the back steps just daydreaming. Back then, what was possible did not matter. I want them to go back there and reconnect with their early, positive daydreaming of what they imagined could be.

As a result, I have repeatedly seen talents blossom. One lady is pursuing ballet; another is representing herself in court in a lawsuit against her abuser; a third is drawing brilliant political cartoons for several newspapers. They all have untouched, unrealized talents that are now undergoing exploration. These abilities, of course, add more information about the real self.

The participants are encouraged to comfort one another, not by advice-giving but by acceptance, and very often a barrage of hugs.

Recently, a dear lady in our group who was struggling in great pain has grown to trust. She was helped to understand that it was her *first* rape, at 15, that caused the second, that caused the third, and so on. Rapists are predators, and predators, by their very nature, go after wounded prey. Vultures can spot disabled targets from a very great distance in the sky.

Abusers as Predators

The same is true of all abusers. They prey on the wounded. One man now in treatment just had to know—was driven to know—why his adoptive father hated him but not his siblings. The answer is quite direct: His siblings had never been wounded, but this boy had been. He had spent his first two years of life in neglectful foster care before being adopted. By the time of his adoption, the main vulture in his life had him well-marked for the kill.

Tracing the Wires and the Inner Voice

Those members of the group who have proven that they feel safe enough to interact are often asked about any present distress. Then the current hurt is traced to an original message communicated in some way in childhood. We ask the question, "What is this pain wired to?" They are taught to visualize actual wires connecting their present discomfort to a real event earlier and, importantly, to the *person* at the end of the wire.

They learn to identify whose voice they hear when they believe they are themselves inflicting the pain. They name the voice when they are compelled to put themselves down or harm themselves, and they come to appreciate the "magical power" of the phantom "renting space" in their heads. They are helped to defy the commands of the abuser's voice and are rewarded with lavish applause and affection every time they disobey. When they feel terror or helplessness, we ask which lie they are honoring.

On and on, they continue their search for the inner child, the real self, before the sacred product underwent tampering. They are not looking for a new person, but an old one who remains young: the person they already are but have yet to realize and celebrate.

As previously explained, when prisoners of war are released, they do not run for freedom but stay huddled at the center of the camp. Freeing the prisoners is not sufficient. Having them grasp the reality of their freedom, that they are already free, is what restores their liberty.

So it is with domestic abuse survivors. They remain prisoners of lies because the truth has not reached their hearts. They crouch in fear, loathing not themselves but who they think they are. They are unaware that the real self is alive and available for wondrous exploration.

They are just waking from slumber and wiping their eyes as they only peek at the light one small glimpse at a time. Now they merely sense an opening, but one day, they will walk out the door if they are given a means of self-discovery.

The Shortcomings of Twelve-Step Programs.

The most serious shortcoming of Twelve-Step programs including Alcoholics Anonymous, Overeaters Anonymous, Narcotics Anonymous and dozen knockoffs is that they don't work except in rare cases. The reason is that they fail to address the cause of addiction, which is almost always child abuse, mostly sexual abuse. Twelve-Step programs will never change; will never respond to this failure, because it becomes a religion for those who take the program seriously. Getting these groups to change at all would be as difficult as getting a fundamentalist to change the Bible.

The program blames "character defects" as the cause of addiction, if anyone would admit a cause. But the general consensus is that addiction arises from nowhere, and the only way to arrest the disease, that is, prevent relapse, is to follow the program with the deepest possible devotion.

Recently, the General Services Office of Alcoholics Anonymous in New York City issued a report to counter a number of studies placing AA's success rate at 5 percent or below. In the report, GSOAA claims a 50 to 75 percent success rate and states quite fairly that the dismal data do not take into account some factors that are difficult, if not impossible, to measure.

For one thing, the studies do not count the number of people who return to the program after leaving nor the number of people who attend reluctantly by court order or to please a family member. Statisticians also cannot measure to what degree the participants are faithfully practicing the program. As the slogan goes, "It works if you work it."

The following facts are provided with the permission of the Gambling Addiction Treatment Services (GATS) Recovery Program in Southern Australia:

> A document prepared by the Mental Health Association in New York State Inc. indicates the degree to which the connection between sexual abuse and later-life drug addiction or alcoholism has been observed in a number of research efforts.
>
> - 75 percent of women in treatment programs for drug and alcohol abuse report having been sexually abused. (*American Journal on Addictions*, June 1997).
>
> - Nearly 90 percent of women who have become dependent upon alcohol suffered severe violence at the hands of a parent or were sexually abused during childhood. (*Journal of Traumatic Stress*, December 1997).
>
> - A study of 100 adult patients with polytoxic drug abuse revealed that 70 percent of the female subjects had been

sexually abused prior to the age of 16. (*Schizophrenia Research*, December 2002).

These findings are supported by an April 2002 "NIDA Notes" document that is posted on the website of the National Institute on Drug Abuse. In that article, writer Patrick Zickler reports that being sexually abused as a child increases the risk that a woman will develop a drug dependence or other addictions later in life:

Using data gathered from interviews of 1,411 adult twins, Dr. Kenneth Kendler and his colleagues [at the Medical College of Virginia Commonwealth University in Richmond] assessed the association between three levels of childhood sex abuse (nongenital, genital, and intercourse) and six adult disorders— major depression, generalized anxiety disorder, panic disorder, bulimia nervosa, alcohol dependence, and drug dependence.

Women who experienced any type of sexual abuse in childhood were roughly three times more likely than non-abused girls to report drug dependence as adults.

"Overall, childhood sexual abuse was more strongly associated with drug or alcohol dependence than with any of the psychiatric disorders," Dr. Kendler says. "Only drug and alcohol dependence were significantly associated with all levels of abuse."

Sexual Assault and Addiction

This issue is complicated because the use of substances may have preceded the assault, occurred during the assault, or developed as a coping strategy in response to the trauma the victim experienced; all yielding potentially different responses and reactions for the victim and by society at large.

Regardless of when the substances were consumed, this topic is further complicated by the fact that substance abuse and victimization both carry a great deal of social stigma in and of themselves, and when a survivor holds both, the stigma can be especially difficult to overcome.

The stigma that is associated with rape, or any sexual assault, and addiction can be a significant obstacle to treatment because of the prevalence with which sexual assault is associated with drug or alcohol abuse:

- Rape victims are 5.3 times more likely than non-victims to have used prescription drugs non-medically.

- Rape victims are 3.4 times more likely to have used marijuana than non-victims.
- Victims of rape are six times more likely to have used cocaine or meth than are women who were not raped.
- Compared to women who had not been raped, rape victims were 10.1 times more likely to have used "hard drugs".

What Are the Twelve Steps?

The Twelve Steps established by AA (and mimicked by others) are as follows:

1. We admitted we were powerless over alcohol—that our lives had become unmanageable.
2. Came to believe that a Power greater than ourselves could restore us to sanity.
3. Made a decision to turn our will and our lives over to the care of God *as we understood Him.*
4. Made a searching and fearless moral inventory of ourselves.
5. Admitted to God, to ourselves, and to another human being the exact nature of our wrongs.
6. Were entirely ready to have God remove all these defects of character.
7. Humbly asked Him to remove our shortcomings.
8. Made a list of all persons we had harmed, and became willing to make amends to them all.
9. Made direct amends to such people wherever possible, except when to do so would injure them or others.
10. Continued to take personal inventory, and when we were wrong, promptly admitted it.
11. Sought through prayer and meditation to improve our conscious contact with God *as we understood Him*, praying only for knowledge of His will for us and the power to carry that out.
12. Having had a spiritual awakening as the result of these steps, we tried to carry this message to alcoholics, and to practice these principles in all our affairs.

Steps 2, 3, and 11 as commonly practiced encourage idolatry. The groups emphasize that anything can be your "higher power" as long as you appoint one, perhaps the group itself, but even an inanimate object such as a chair. It is as though belief itself is curative on its own, regardless of what the belief pertains to. Believing in a thing is as valuable as belief in God.

Steps 4 through 10 are nothing less than devastating to a victim of abuse, who already blames himself for every offense ever committed against him (or her). Many victims of sexual abuse visualize themselves as snakes, vampires, or rats; so great is there self-loathing. No wonder AA and similar programs fail miserably. They hammer the nails deeper and deeper even though every abuse victim has already crucified himself daily for years. When a court sentences a drug offender to attend these meetings, the punishment is far worse than jail. It is inhumane.

The New 7-Step Program

The reader will notice that the words alcohol, drugs, or addiction are not mentioned at all in this new program. The reason is that these substances are not the problem. Until one discovers who he really is, he has little hope of giving up the self-medication which has given him the only comfort he has in a world that long ago has rejected him. The abused substance has become his best, and usually his only, friend. If he has a sense of self at all, it is grossly distorted and far from what God intended.

The Lord's Prayer

Each meeting, whether daily or weekly, begins with the Lord's Prayer, followed by an invitation to the Holy Spirit. I want to share my personal understanding, phrase by phrase, of why the Lord's Prayer is perfect for victims of child or domestic abuse.

"Our Father": He is our father, and has been before the creation of the world. He was our father before we reached our mother's womb. He is everyone's father, whether realized or not. He will always be our father and will always protect us and provide all that we need.

St. Paul implied that Jesus wants us to think of His father as our "Daddy", even though He is the Almighty God of all. We may call Him "Abba", the kind of father whose knee we can sit on, embrace, and receive security and comfort—most of all, the kind of father who deserves our greatest love.

"...who art in Heaven": He is in Heaven. That is His residence—a real location that is both physical and spiritual but that has no bounds. It is beyond both vast and beautiful, for it is perfect. And it is our future home. His Son has prepared a place for us in one of His many mansions.

The word "mansion" is a term we can understand, but it cannot begin to describe the dwellings there. If you have ever been overcome by beauty of any kind, you will be constantly overwhelmed by beauty of every kind.

Even though He does reside in Heaven, He is yet with us on Earth by His Spirit, whom His Son and He have sent to be with us always.

"Hallowed be Thy name": This statement has two meanings. One, His name is truly hallowed, or "holy", and two, it must be regarded as holy by all people. Also, we are praying that every knee shall bow at the utterance of His name.

I do not mean that all should get on their knees every time He is mentioned, but He does command that His name be used only with the utmost reverence. Using His name carelessly, without being conscious of who He is—or worse, speaking it in anger or as a form of cursing—is in itself accursed! The same is true for the name of His Son.

"Thy kingdom come": We are praying at least two things. First, that His holy kingdom be established on Earth, and second, that His kingdom be expressed in us. His Son told us that the kingdom is within us and among us.

It is His will that His people call on Him to bring His kingdom soon. There will be no peace, no justice, and no end to suffering of every kind, until His kingdom arrives. When we pray these words, we are praying for the early, triumphant return of the Son.

"Thy will be done on Earth as it is in heaven": There is no higher request than for His will to be done. We are asking for His will to be done in all things, but especially in us. We are also asking for the grace to be able to know and do His will.

We cannot know the fullness of His will, but we can discover His will for us if we ask sincerely and persistently but most importantly allowing plenty of daily time to listen.

When we pray for His will, we are asking for every good thing in one request, for His will proceeds from nothing other than perfect love. Such is the largest and most comprehensive supplication of all.

Also, when we thus pray, we are surrendering ourselves to Him. We are sacrificing our own will so that it can be replaced with His will. This is what we pray and should pray.

"Give us this day our daily bread..." Here we are asking for something He does without ceasing. But we are acknowledging that He is the provider of all that we need. We are asking not only for food which nourishes the body and for other necessities of life, but for the Bread of Life.

We are praying for the Lord's Supper. "You must eat this bread and drink this cup if you are to have life in you," His Son has told us. Because only His Church can provide this sustenance, we are thereby praying for the Church, which is His Body. We are praying for the "bread from heaven", which is the Christ, and from Whom we must partake often.

"...and forgive us our trespasses as we forgive those who trespass against us": We are asking not only for the forgiveness of our many sins, but also that He forgives us in direct proportion to the pardon we grant others. The more we forgive, the more we will be forgiven. If we are wise, we should be literally searching for people to forgive, for the sins of us all are great.

When our anger or resentment is so strong that we have great difficulty forgiving someone, then we should pray for the grace and the power. The power to forgive must be given. It is not in us by nature.

And how do we forgive? We pray for those who stir up ill feelings within us. The Son has already said, "Pray for your enemies." Again, when we find this difficult, we should pray for the power and for the willingness.

"Lead us not into temptation, but deliver us from evil": Many have wondered about this wording and asked themselves why God would lead us into evil. Certainly He would not. Never. This petition is for Him to lead us away from temptation.

As we all know, temptations are everywhere in this world, and we all have been subject to most of them. We cannot fight them on our own. We must have His help. We need His grace.

It is the Liar who places in our minds the justification to give in to sin. So when we pray, "...deliver us from evil" we are asking His protection against the lies of the Enemy and the awesome power of the Enemy. The Serpent deceived Eve with a lie and Adam with a rationalization. And they were not born in sin; they acquired a sin nature through their disobedience. We, however, were born with a sin nature. How much more at risk are we?

We should never try to resist evil on our own. We cannot succeed. The Father has given us a Savior, and He has taught us how to pray.

Remember, it is because He loves us that He does not want us to sin. The Ten Commandments, and the laws that proceeded from them, are not for His benefit but for ours.

"For thine is the kingdom, the power and the glory forever and ever": These words did not come from Jesus but were added after the Reformation. It is just as well for Him if we omit these, I think. Besides, the grammar is incorrect. The word "is" should be "are" or "art".

"Amen": So may these things be.

Prayer to the Holy Spirit

Holy Spirit, we welcome you. Come to be with us. Guide our thoughts, our words, and our hearts, for You are the only Healer. Amen.

The 7 Steps

Step 1. We came to realize at the deepest level that we have believed lies about ourselves due to the damaging influence of other people and horrifying events. Some of us thought of ourselves as snakes, vampires, rats, and other despicable things. We came to see that our ideas about ourselves were robbing us of a happy, fulfilling life; that our souls had been wounded.

Step 2. When we felt safe, when we really wanted to, we shared our hurts and wounds with the group and found that they understood our pain. This sharing made clear that when we had been violated by other people, it was not our fault but theirs.

Step 3. We became keenly aware of other critically important facts that would help direct our lives:

- That God is the only One Who knows who we are; that no one on Earth is qualified to judge us or tell us anything about the kind of people we are inside;

- That we must develop a healthy relationship with our Creator so that He would show us who we are in fact; that studying the Holy Scripture and other sacred writings can help us to know Him;

- That every human being, without a single exception, has been born for one reason: the will of God, because He wanted us here on Earth regardless of how we were conceived and no matter who our parents are.

Step 4. We learned that every person who believes in God has a calling, a job to do, and that we must find our calling by asking God in prayer persistently until we have the answer; thus, we found our calling, which put us on the path to discovering our true selves. We were greatly comforted by the fact that our suffering had meaning and value; that it contributed to our calling in a vital way and helped to describe our true identity.

Step 5. We discovered that God's nature is perfect love; therefore, it is an undeniable fact that He loves each one of us unconditionally; and:

- That no one can understand God completely but that He has revealed to mankind many wondrous things about Himself and that He is constantly revealing more to those who seek Him daily through prayer and study;

- That we are not born with a natural capacity to love God but that He will give us this ability if we ask; that we can learn to love Him back.

Step 6. We resolved to live our lives as brand-new people, feeling re-created when we found our own souls at long last. When we saw that who we thought we were was false, we took off our old image of ourselves and dropped it like an old coat, never to pick it up again. We committed our real selves to a joyful, fulfilling life of giving love and making each day a celebration.

Step 7. We kept our souls nourished by prayer, thanksgiving, worship, and study. Many of us were blessed to find a church or synagogue with a well-educated and dedicated pastor who had validly been called to his vocation.

A recent patient, a 22-year-old man, had been addicted to oxycodone since his early teens. He was unaware that he had ever been abused. But when he took my Inventory for Concealed Child Abuse, using a red pen, the pages looked like they were bleeding! [This test can easily be adapted for adults.]

When in time he came to realize the cause of all of his other symptoms, he was thoroughly relieved and thanked me again and again. The most remarkable outcome is that he made a decision to give up drugs, even though I had never suggested that he do so. With my help, he visited a physician who put him on a drug that relieves withdrawal symptoms and the craving but does not cause euphoria.

For the first time in a very long while, he got a job, and his employer is very pleased with his work. He is saving toward buying a used car. His total treatment at this writing has consisted of four visits. This young man is living proof that when the real problem is dealt with, results quickly follow.

14 | Special Populations

Discussed in this chapter are two of the groups most vulnerable to child abuse: inner-city children living in gross impoverishment, both economically and culturally; and those children with attention-deficit hyperactivity disorder (ADHD). We will also cover what should be done for the huge number of alcoholics and other drug addicts, people with PTSD, prostitutes, and souls starving in church.

Cultural Deprivation

Of all the minority groups in the United States, Black children trapped in a "ghetto" mentality are the most subject to every kind of child abuse. Their high-risk status arises from cultural deprivation as a result of the present generation still living the effects of slavery that supposedly ended with the Civil War. Although the war made slavery illegal, it did not remove the generational effects.

Slavery utterly destroyed the black family. Men and women were kept in separate barracks, and not even partnerships were permitted, let alone marriages. Men and women were forced to "mate" like animals. Plantation owners were breeders of beings they did not consider human. The masters "reared" the offspring only in the sense of teaching obedience to the master.

Because slavery continued for generations, the captives, when set free after the war, had no concept of a black family. They had never seen one nor heard of one. They did not even know that they could form such a thing as a family.

Bigotry continues long after the abolishment of slavery, and right up to the present day. Only in very recent years has this population had an opportunity for education. Even now it is only theoretically possible for every black citizen to receive an education.

The fact that the "fences are down" has not fully penetrated the pockets of deep, long-lasting poverty within the inner city of every major metropolitan area.

One might assume that small children encountered in these neighborhoods would be found to be hostile. However, the fact is that the predominant mood is shame. Among older people, the norm is serious religious conviction, a kind and compassionate "mellowness", and an absence of bitterness over having lived a restricted life. If we look at the very young and the old, we find Blacks, even in these conditions, to be gentle people. In every age group, blacks are more hygienically clean than the majority of the population in the U.S. Even fierce gang members are freshly bathed and well-groomed.

I have formed these observations through years of working with AIDS victims in a program I began in order to serve them at home. Day after day, I entered such sections of Jacksonville, Florida, and encountered people of all ages. Even the teenagers became friendly, when they knew I was there to help. This is not to say that I was not frightened at first, because I was. White people are afraid of Black people, and they have good reason to be.

Somewhere deep down in every decent white, there is a realization, though it may be covered up, that our ancestors caused these conditions in the first place and allowed them to prevail. Further, it is a fact that more crimes, except for white-collar, are committed by blacks, as the daily newspapers and TV keep reminding us. The time is generations overdue for the white man to ask *why*; then to ask *what can be done?*

Even though this is not a good time to begin change, with families of every color on the endangered list, we must begin. Ours must be the generation that helps. Part of the "why" has already been described. Blacks have lacked a family structure. Even though today single-parent families are very prevalent in the white population, as are "partnerships", these phenomena have produced dire consequences for Blacks. The absence of a father is child neglect at its worst.

The greater the poverty, the greater the shame of the small children in the Black population. What else could we expect to see? We know already that neglect or other abuse results in the child's taking the blame on himself. Black children begin their lives believing that they already have all that they deserve. Their predicament is *cultural abuse*.

When they enter school, they must face head-on the reality that they are not wanted there, that at least some people don't like them, are afraid of them, or even hate them. The greatest struggle of all begins when the experimental becoming of adolescence arrives.

Without a father, the Black male teen has no "welcome to manhood". Yet he is male, and he knows that whatever his identity, it must conform to what his idea of male is. By prior example, therefore, he begins this stage of development with guidelines that have never worked. He sees adult males in any deprived culture impregnate women as though they are doing them a favor and then disappear. He sees grandmothers raising children, while the mothers go out and work at very low-level jobs. He sees his white schoolmates enjoying a much higher standard of living, and comes to the solid realization that he has been cheated.

Adolescent development largely takes the form of protest and defiance. Why should he honor the rules of such a society? The process of development propels him to find further identity plus an experimental personality that will work in the peer group. But the peers he must join and be accepted by are also defiant, and many are enraged. His clique fights with others and commits crimes.

Contrary to white teens, the Black youngster has a very constricted choice of cliques. There is little likelihood that he will find a solidly-established group of Black teen scholars, although thankfully, he may find a group of athletes. But even if he identifies with the athletes, and is accepted, what about his mind? Where is the opportunity for him to be nourished intellectually so that he may become a desperately needed leader one day?

The process is quite similar with adolescent girls in the inner-city culture. Many have the idea that being impregnated by a boy is a compliment, even an honor, although he remains in her life only for a short time. Her education is interrupted in order to work at a fast-food restaurant while her mother raises the child. Not only that, but her own mother may have been through many rotating boyfriends, a certain percentage of whom have been abusive. Taking abuse from a male and being abandoned is a normal part of being a woman. Having a child is all a girl needs.

Many thousands of men and women have overcome these obstacles and achieved a fulfilling life. They have done their part to stop the cycle. But thousands of exceptions are still not enough, because only a very few are communicators who attempt to bring change within their own community. Not since Dr. Martin Luther King has there been a spokesman with as much charisma and *courage* to make a significant difference in the hope level of the deprived portion of the black culture. Thankfully, Mr. Herman Cain has come upon the national scene and has acquired respect by every U.S. cultural group. He is a very, very great blessing to us all (Cain, 2011).

Hope is needed more than anything. Next to that is education targeted specifically at changing the mindset of the ghetto. It is very significant that values and character are starting to be taught in public schools. But not until the present generation of parents and grandparents understands the "why", and what can be done, will there be visible improvement in this plight.

Black ministers, elected officials, physicians, educators and other professionals must become vocal and speak specifically to the problem: the absence of family and, more exactly, the mindset of teens.

Whites should attempt to overcome their fear and mistrust of Blacks by facing the real danger: what will happen to us all if the black family remains unformed and the white family follows the same path. Our society has a greater danger than crime: we face extinction unless the family is reformed on solid ground. If the American family does not make a comeback, our country is doomed.

Every white person in power, including members of the news media, should be in search of Black spokespersons and should offer every possible opportunity for them to convey these messages. Black supervisors in industry should be afforded plentiful opportunities to speak to their workforce.

Popular music groups and movie stars should be outspoken about the issues, not by endless complaining about injustice, as real as it is, but by addressing in the most forceful way the solutions.

The white community must change its attitude. Some researchers have tried to prove a difference in intelligence levels between the two races but have ended up with well-deserved egg on their faces. The greatest resource in the entire world is all but untapped: the enormous population of black people and the inestimable contribution they have already made and can make further to the benefit of us all.

Anyone examining science, the professions, music, drama, writing, business, and the arts in general—or any other field—must admit that we have a priceless resource in the Black community that has already emerged but can, in the future, blossom even more in every institution and setting throughout the world.

Obviously, the United States is not the only nation with the far-reaching problem of cultural deprivation. Our church endorses as one of our ministries The Beautiful Heart Foundation, headed by Anacleto B. Millendez, M.D. He is a medical missionary to the Philippines, where extreme poverty is rampant. He delivers not only medical care, with medicines donated by pharmaceutical companies, but he provides education with a solid spiritual base.

Dr. Millendez teaches children and adults how to discover their talents and develop them as a way out of poverty. He has a great talent for instilling initiative. A devoted Catholic, as are most Filipinos, he builds grottos and other places of worship in remote islands. Recently he established a mission on the very island where the first Christians landed in Asia nearly 500 years ago. Presently, he is working toward offering his ministry to impoverished people in California.

Attention-Deficit Hyperactivity Disorder

Nearly 30 years ago, I noticed an obscure little article in an esoteric journal that discussed this subject, ADHD. I cannot find a reference to it, although I have searched everywhere, and none of my colleagues have ever heard of it either. If the author will come forward, due reference and credit will be given. What I do know is that the premise of that piece is very, very true.

In taking that small amount of information and adding my experience with children over all these years, I have come to believe that this condition is physiological and *not* psychological. It has become a "garbage-can" diagnosis overly used when an evaluator has not looked for causality, so that many children with this label do not have this condition at all but are instead suffering from PTSD as the result of child abuse.

Actual ADHD, according to my experience, is caused by sensory deprivation or restriction of movement during the period from infancy to about age 3. I have yet to find a case of this condition where a child has not either undergone some necessary medical procedure or suffered abuse resulting in one or more of the major senses being blocked for a prolonged period of immobilization. Many an accident has also caused such blocking.

Interfering with the perceptive senses or movement produces an "overcharged" central nervous system, whereby energy continues to build until there is an outlet. When this physiological change occurs, it remains permanent throughout the lifespan. The result is that movement and perceptual stimulation are required in excess. If these are not supplied at frequent intervals, the child becomes irritable, then angry, and finally enraged.

Besides hyperactivity, the constellation of symptoms includes being stubborn, having a "short fuse" when it comes to temper, defiance, and a strong liking for very loud music or other noise, as well as every form of physical stimulation, including touch. This may include very hot or very cold showers and back rubs; and activities that stimulate any of the senses, such as video games, sports, and almost any kind of exercise.

Some of the leading causes are surgery during infancy that requires strapping the baby down; orthopedic corrective devices, such as bars; prolonged confinement to an incubator; and even a difficult delivery whereby the baby is trapped in the birth canal. Tubes in the ears to correct hearing infections, procedures done to the eyes, and immobilization of any part of the body or the entire body are also included.

Why these procedures have this effect is not known. It is my understanding that when ulcer medications were being researched, it became necessary to produce ulcers in laboratory animals in order to test the trial medication. Researchers found that if they tied together the hind legs of any laboratory animal soon after birth, then an ulcer would develop within two or three days. Importantly, it was noted that the animal behaved in a hyperactive manner and further, that in later months, it was not able to learn the tasks that the other animals learned, such as pushing a lever for a food pellet. Still more importantly, the animals thus restrained as newborns remained with these handicaps for the remainder of their lives.

Obviously, the animals did not have a psychological or emotional problem; they were not mentally ill. They had undergone a physiological change that altered their central nervous system.

With children, stimulation at very frequent intervals is an absolute necessity. For example, a young man in his junior year of high school had a life-long ambition of attending a certain university. Because of this condition, however, he was in trouble most of the time, and he could not concentrate in class. He was failing. No matter how hard he tried, he was not able to stay focused in the classroom nor even to sit still.

He had been born prematurely and thus had been confined to an incubator for weeks. Not only that, but he was immobilized inside the device so that feeding tubes and the like would remain in place. All of his life, he had been hyperactive and easily angered, but once he "exploded", he would settle down quickly. He loved burning-hot showers and loud music. By early adolescence, he had gotten very down on himself because he seemed to be irritable most of the time. He was ashamed of himself and felt tremendous guilt over snapping at his parents and siblings.

When it was revealed to him that his problem was physical and not mental—further, that he was not responsible—there were tears of relief. I instructed him to get a portable radio with headphones and to play it every time he started to become irritable; also to take plenty of hot showers and to ask his mother to rub his back.

But the most important thing I did for this young man was to talk to an open-minded and cooperative counselor at his high school. She issued him a special pass that allowed him to go outside and run around the entire school building between classes.

The results were optimum. In fact, he did graduate with a grade average sufficient for admission to the university of his choice. Once he was in college, he had much more freedom and knew well what to do for himself; that is, how to manage his condition.

Many times I have asked an unbelieving mother in my office to take her son (or daughter), who was running around the room, and begin to scratch his back. Time after time, the child would settle down. Then I would have the child do some jumping jacks until he felt tired. When the stimulation and exercise had been completed, the child behaved normally. I must repeat, however, that such measures are required on an hourly basis or more, depending on severity.

Some experimentation is required to find the most effective form of stimulation. One 10-year-old boy, when he became wildly out of control, could be calmed only by hot showers.

One might ask why this topic is included in this book. One reason is that hyperactive children receive more abuse than those without this problem. More importantly, however, it must be pointed out that neglect can easily produce this life-long condition. A child not fed when hungry is deprived of the sense of taste, and the strong sense of hunger goes unsatisfied. Similarly, a child confined to a crib is denied full movement, as is a child forced to remain in a stroller or high chair long beyond his endurance. Some children are locked in closets or tied down as punishment.

In short, a parent who purposely does not meet a child's needs as they occur is committing neglect. All needs are naturally occurring, and neither a child nor an adult can control when a need will arise. Because children cannot meet their own needs, a parent must. All kinds of consequences can follow when needs are not met.

Alcoholics and Other Addicts

Jacksonville, Florida, is blessed with a nonprofit organization, Gateway Community Services, which provides free medical detoxification services covering both alcohol and other drugs. Medications are used in a protocol lasting about 10 days for alcohol and longer for other drugs. The medications are slowly reduced in a controlled, in-patient environment. The patients remain relatively comfortable during their detoxification.

Unfortunately, the in-patients are treated as prisoners, to some degree. Even though they are fed well, and the surroundings are kept very clean, they must dress in orange jumpsuits. They are allowed to go outside under supervision several times a day but only for a short period of time. Generally, the staff consists of nonprofessional "babysitters" plus one registered nurse on duty and a physician on call who also does a physical exam for each new intake.

Because Gateway does provide very valuable life-saving services, I hesitate to criticize. But I might say that the untrained staff members could be a lot more pleasant and respectful to the patients, and the orange jumpsuits could readily be done away with, to be replaced by the patient's own clothing (if he or she has any). A TV that is large enough to be viewed by a group could also be provided along with books and magazines because there is much idle time to be filled. The most serious problem, however, is that each patient is required to attend AA twice a day. That subject has already been covered.

My main point is that every city with a large population should have such a facility. However, AA is the only model of treatment. The same is true for almost every private rehab, even the most exclusive. Therefore a private facility may have a better appearance and many more amenities, but the devastating effects of the AA model will be forced into the wounds of abuse victims.

Legalize Doctors, Not Drugs

As the debate rages on, whether or not to legalize all drugs, another idea has not yet emerged, and that is to legalize doctors. What I mean is that since addiction is a disease, why not pull out all stops and allow every licensed physician to care for his addicted patients? Why should a doctor be disciplined for writing repeated prescriptions for cocaine, heroin, or any other drug to which his or her patient is addicted? It is insane not to allow doctors to give the same quality of care to his addicted patients as he gives to all his other patients.

The American Medical Association must come to realize that when they tie the hands of a physician in this regard, they deny doctors the chance to save lives. Yes, save lives. Many addicts die from their disease from unintentional overdosing or by ingesting drugs that are contaminated, mixed with unknown poisons, or injected with dirty needles. In addition, they kill people.

If doctors were permitted to do their jobs without fear of recrimination, pharmaceutical companies would certainly follow suit and manufacture high-quality drugs. They would also compete with each other with the effect of establishing reasonable prices.

Quality-controlled disposable needles could be dispensed at pharmacies. Professional pharmacists would continue their vital role of backup by warning the patient of dangerous conflicts with other medicines and would give other precautions that they routinely provide. They are very well educated in pharmacology, more than any other profession.

It is a fact that rates of violent crime, especially murder, do dramatically plummet in countries where drugs have already been legalized. No one can deny that the statistics prove this very principle, study after study. Why are we being so absolutely stupid?

Gang violence, burglaries, store robberies, and other drug-related crime would become exceptions in a civilized society rather than the prevailing rule that afflicts the entire population now. By restricting doctors we have given free rein to a pandemic that is far worse than the enormous problems caused by prohibition of alcohol. When alcohol became legal, it did not become safe, but the country's safety was indeed increased. The very same will become the case if physicians are again allowed to practice medicine.

We should put aside the endless arguments about who is to blame for someone being an addict and concentrate on treating what has long ago been defined as a disease by the AMA.

Instead of putting our tax dollars toward feeding and housing prisoners who are not criminals plus maintaining prisons and building more facilities, we could develop treatment centers that are effective. Many minimum-security prisons could easily be remodeled for this new purpose.

Addicts who spend all of their time doing whatever is necessary to get their drugs could actually be employed and pay taxes! Even those with the most hardened hearts on this issue would have to agree that this idea would have huge financial benefits. For those who really care about addicts and good medical practice, the solution is so simple: Let doctors practice medicine!

Prostitutes

There may be one somewhere in the world, but I doubt that there are more than only a few prostitutes who are not victims of child sexual abuse. The self-loathing is so pervasive that a child—yes, a child—or an adult in this occupation has no trouble being humiliated for money. They provide not only sex but an outlet for the kind of sadistic treatment that sociopaths cherish.

Predators seeking for a child prostitute should be legally punished with very great severity. But the child should be rescued and treated professionally as well as placed in a carefully selected foster home.

Adult prostitution should be legalized. I say this not because I believe in immorality but because our present policies are inhumane. These women suffer enough without being harassed by the police. Besides, they are usually released soon after the arrest, with the result that police are wasting their time, which ought to be valuable. They should be stopping violent crime.

When our country was founded, the fathers based their system of law on English common law, which itself was adapted from Eleventh-Century Catholic Canon Law (Hartman et al, 2012). In common law, if there is no victim, there is no crime. We would do well as a nation to return to this principle.

In those parts of Nevada where prostitution has been legalized, women receive medical check-ups four times a year. It is a crime if they knowingly pass on a disease, especially a sexually transmitted one. They receive as much police protection as any other citizen and are provided healthcare.

Despite the debasement, prostitutes derive a sad benefit in their work. They conclude that they must be worth something if men will pay money to be with them. Society should be as merciful to a prostitute as we are to other victims of abuse. I repeat what I have said more than once: there is no normal way to react to craziness. Prostitution is a reaction to the atrocity of child sexual abuse.

They should be offered treatment for the abuse they suffered as a child, and they should be offered treatment if they are supporting a drug habit by selling themselves. Unfortunately, as previously stated, there are very few psychotherapists who know how to treat the aftermath of abuse.

Souls Starving in Church

In discussing this subject, I must first put forth my bias: I am a Catholic, and in fact, the Metropolitan Archbishop of the Holy Catholic Church International.

Catholics and Jews have an important commonality; that is, education. Rabbis and priests have a very high level of learning going well beyond the bachelor's-degree level. They are life-long students and valued teachers who instruct the faithful with an authority based on knowledge acquired through very hard work. Many have earned their doctorates in theology.

There is a moral problem in this country that is contributing to the rapid decay of our civilization. A great number of professed Christians and Jews have lost their thirst for the eternal truths that are supposed to underlie and govern the way we live. Some have grown lukewarm and others have grown cold.

I believe that God gives every man and woman an opportunity to accept a *love* of the truth—not the truth itself, for it must be sought, but a love of it. Some accept this offer, some reject it outright, and others lose this love of the truth without awareness that it is fading. Just as a frog in slowly heated water doesn't notice that it's being killed, so people who do not nourish this love begin to starve spiritually without the slightest recognition.

"Feel-good religion" is a cancer growing in America, a disease in force so long that one can measure the impact. There are charts indicating the rise of crime following the removal of prayer from public schools. The graph is a nearly straight line running upwards to the top right of the scale. Religious people permitted the government to take their rights away. Religious people allow abortion to be legal rather than screaming bloody murder for as long as it would take to get the godless Supreme Court to overturn its ruling.

The only thing supreme about this court is its name. With a few exceptions, the present members are a gang of murderers with black robes on—robes that should have a hood attached to cover a shameful face for not protecting human life.

The expression "contempt of court" has great significance for me: I have nothing but contempt for some of the decisions this group has made, although as an American, I must honor this branch of government. The only reason I oppose capital punishment is that I cannot place complete trust in the court system, even at the local level.

Neither do I trust a pastor who, in his ignorance, entertains his congregation instead of teaching them the truth—the truth according to Holy Scripture, held sacred by Jews and Christians alike.

There is no sense of the holy in the churches that are thriving the fastest. They look more like auditoriums than a holy place where God dwells in a special way. In Jacksonville, one mega-church must employ a team of technicians at $40 an hour each to prepare for every service, before and after. Another church here requires for membership that a document be signed to enable automatic withdrawal of 10 percent of every paycheck deposit. Its administrative building alone is six stories high.

There is a complete absence of a sacramental life even though the sacraments are one of God's favorite ways of feeding the soul directly. All of the seven sacraments were instituted by Jesus Himself and are described in Holy Scripture. Three of the main ones are baptism, the Lord's Supper, and matrimony.

A sacrament, consisting of a set combination of words and acts, is an outward sign of an inner blessing with strong, lasting power. For example, baptism and circumcision make a baby a member of God's family. That is why Catholics, Lutherans, and Episcopalians plus Orthodox believers baptize their babies soon after birth. The Jewish practice is for circumcision to take place on the eighth day after birth.

Since the earliest days of Christianity, infant baptism has been considered an absolute necessity according to the teachings of Jesus Himself.

He said that all must be born again of water and of the spirit, and taught emphatically that we should allow the little children to come to Him for they exemplify the kingdom of heaven. The term "little children" includes infants according to the Aramaic dialect spoken by Christ.

It is by this first of the seven sacraments that one becomes a citizen of the Kingdom of God and at the same time receives his first infusion of grace (unearned favor). The taint of original sin is removed thereby, and the child is thus enabled to accept the revealed truth to which he will be exposed throughout his life.

In other words, the infant is made capable of recognizing, understanding, and choosing the teachings of Christ as he comes to discover them. His free will to choose right from wrong is unleashed from the blinding shackles of being born in sin, as we all are. He becomes able to see and to accept.

If we are to interpret the words of our Lord correctly, it is the Father's will that all men be saved, regardless of age. And Jesus clearly showed us that the first door to salvation is baptism.

For nearly 1600 years, the above teachings were universally believed by the Christian church. Conversely, the teaching that one must be of a reasonable age to make such a commitment on his own, voluntarily, after already being saved, is a diversion from ancient truth and is also illogical.

If an infant, for example, were to be relocated when his family moves from Kansas to Pennsylvania, would he be less a citizen of the new state because he has no understanding of what has taken place? Or when a Jewish child is circumcised on the eighth day of life, is he not circumcised because he did not comprehend?

Old Testament obedience to the Law of Moses is a precursor to the New Testament observance of the Messiah's requirements. It is therefore not at all unreasonable to compare Jewish circumcision to Christian baptism. Christ said that He did not come to abolish the law but to fulfill it.

Moses required that newborns be presented in the temple, and Jesus warns that infants must be made citizens of heaven by baptism at the earliest feasible time. Such is the fulfillment of God's law.

In light of history, the teaching that this sacrament is merely an act of obedience is relatively new and is not justified by scripture nor tradition. Neither can this error be adopted by any other valid source and most certainly not by reason.

Not Criticizing All Protestants

I do not have these harsh criticisms of mainstream Protestant churches such as Presbyterian, Methodist, Lutheran, and Assembly of God. Their pastors undergo rigorous study which they must complete successfully before they are even considered for ordination. No, my criticism is focused only on what I call "bootleg" churches.

A typical bootleg pastor has no education at all, not even a bachelor's degree in theology or biblical studies. Some are high-school drop-outs. One day out of nowhere, they proclaim that God called them to preach, and people take their word at face value. The pastor is either a fake or is deluded. But if he is a convincing public speaker, he or she gains followers. No one would trust an uneducated, inexperienced surgeon to operate on his body. Yet thousands place their eternal souls in the hands of "pastors" who may not even know how to read and write beyond the eighth-grade level.

These pastors may start off by preaching various parts of the Bible that they like, as they ignore all the rest. But then they compromise and compromise until their congregations begin to grow faster. They follow the peoples' will, not God's. Then they think that their success proves that they have God's favor. The more they grow, the more God loves what they are doing.

This is where societal decay begins, in the church; where souls are starving; where souls are denied real food. They do not have the strength to stand up for what is true. For example, human life is sacred; not only unborn babies, but drug addicts and prostitutes. Marriage is sacred; divorce with remarriage is a very serious sin. Any sex act outside of marriage is a sin. Love of money is idolatry. Being stingy and neglecting a neighbor in need is sinful.

In these churches, evil people can attend in order to keep up the air-tight facade of being good. The "worship" services do not make them uncomfortable because nothing offensive is ever spoken. Nothing is more repulsive to an evil person than the truth.

Almost everybody in the whole world believes that there is such a thing as the soul. Every single religion in recorded history believes in the soul, that it is a living thing continuing to exist after the body dies. All living things require nourishment.

Truth as Food for the Soul

The "food" for the soul is eternal truth. For a soul to grow, every human being requires a steady diet of truth. But the truth is not easily obtained. It does not come from being entertained even if the so-called church has attractive programs for the children and emotionally stirring music.

The truth comes through the hard work of study and through worship characterized by a deep sense of the holy with a sincere regard for reverence. It only stands to reason that if somebody claims to love God, then he would want to know everything about Him that he can. This search is a life-long endeavor that very few people are willing to undertake. They work all week long, so they want to relax on Sunday or Saturday.

Christians in name only and Jews in name only will never gain the strength desperately needed by society right now in order to save our civilization in the United States.

Christians, baptize your children. Jews, circumcise your baby sons. Do what the Old and the New Testaments say, and study to show yourself approved. Search for a church or synagogue where you can sense the presence of God and obtain real food. If you need faith, pray for it. If you love God, learn everything you possibly can about Him.

Remembering the Jewish People

It is crucial for Christians to recall often that our religion stands on the foundation of the Old Testament. We forget that the ancestors of our

Jewish brothers and sisters are the original fathers of our faith. In the Catholic Mass, Abraham is called our "Father in Faith".

Educated Christians understand that Christianity is not a departure from Judaism but a continuation of it; that is, the completion of the Bible story. Without an Old Testament, there could not be a new.

But even with spiritual ties so strong as to make us brothers (and sisters) in faith, we Christians of the world are not completely "there" when it comes to protecting the nation of Israel. At this writing, the President of the United States has agreed to give Israel "bunker busting" bombs only if Israel would postpone any major strike against Iran until after the 2012 Presidential Election. Never mind that Iran can strike Israel within the next few minutes.

What is even more baffling than this absurdity itself is the fact that Americans are not screaming bloody murder. Christians, where are you? Americans, how can you place your brothers and sisters at risk of annihilation?

Professing Christians who do not love the Jewish people, who do not preach their virtues from the pulpit, who do not teach their children to recognize who our true brothers and sisters are, will find themselves in flames as hot as their hearts are cold.

15 The Dangerous Student

It has been stated that in my experience, children who are abused do not grow up to be abusers themselves. However, it is clear that youngsters entering school, as well as those already enrolled, can be explosive. Such is the case because certain individuals, depending on the type of abuse plus their own constitutions can be made mentally ill in a way that can present an imminent danger to the young person himself or to other students, as well as to teachers. Columbine and similar tragedies, another very recently occurring in Canton, Ohio, have taught us this lesson. For these reasons, I have included screenings that can bring attention to students who are suffering and who could possibly be dangerous.

The questionnaires presented are experimental and preliminary. Several prominent institutions are testing these instruments at this writing for reliability and validity. Others are invited. The content validity is derived from 28 years of personal experience by the author and his colleagues, plus generally accepted factors spread throughout the literature.

Student Critical Symptoms Questionnaire

For grades 3 through 12 and 1st year college.

Instructions for Administration

All questions are to be read aloud by the examiner and answered "yes" or "no" by the student. Positive responses indicate a risk to some degree because every question can prompt an abnormal "yes" response.

This is a *preliminary* effort to develop a valid test, but in its present stage of development, it can *give only clues*. The number of positive responses justifying further evaluation by a qualified psychologist has yet to be established. However, the examiner may give added weight to certain responses, according to the examiner's own best judgment, especially if experienced and if familiar with the examinee's history. Questions can be repeated upon request.

Before administration, put the student at ease by explaining that this is a routine test to determine anything special that the school can do to make him/her comfortable. State that this questionnaire may not be necessary in his/her case, but that all students are given this opportunity, especially when new to the school, and that it is for their benefit.

Say to students:

> Here are some questions I'm going to ask. Some may sound strange, but don't let that bother you. Remember that this questionnaire is given to many people, and everybody's background is different. Please answer "yes" or "no", whichever comes to you first. Try not to hesitate. Let's begin. This won't take long."

Questions

1. I have been beaten up.
2. I don't know if I want to be ignored or not.
3. I daydream about getting even.
4. Very few people can understand me.
5. I've been insulted again and again.
6. If people knew my real powers, they'd respect me.
7. Most students are mean.
8. I dreamed I paid back the people who hurt me.
9. I have no reason to respect my teachers.
10. Some people don't deserve to live.
11. My mind has very special powers.
12. There are weapons in my home—at least one.
13. I've thought of using a weapon on my enemies.
14. I don't want to be like other people.
15. If people knew how important I am, they would admire me.
16. I'd feel better if some people left me alone.
17. There's no use talking to my mother or father.
18. I have a brother or sister who gets better treatment than I do.
19. It would suit me fine if I never had to go home.
20. Coming to school is very hard for me.
21. I hate for the other kids to see me naked in the locker room.
22. I think that all people are animals deep down.
23. When I'm home, I rarely come out of my room.
24. There are secrets about me that nobody will ever know.
25. My favorite video or internet games are very violent.
26. I love movies where there's plenty of bloodshed.
27. I'm not loved at home the way most kids are.
28. The way other students act is stupid.
29. There are people who "have it in" for me.
30. Some people are planning bad things for me.
31. I know that one day, I'll get justice.
32. I have powers that people don't know about.
33. I am extremely brilliant, but others can't recognize it.
34. Words can hurt almost as much as physical pain.

35. I try hard to avoid certain people.
36. I freeze in place and don't move for a while.
37. I lose the look on my face so nobody can tell what I'm feeling.
38. I have rolled up in a ball on the floor a lot, or in bed.
39. I have banged my head against the wall or the back of my bed.
40. Some people can read your mind.
41. It's possible to be controlled by somebody else or something else.
42. I daydream or stare off into space a lot.
43. I forget what I'm doing.
44. I don't feel pain when something should hurt.
45. I feel afraid but don't know why.
46. Sometimes I have greater power than anybody.
47. I often feel guilty without knowing why.
48. I worry about my temper.
49. Breaking things in a rage is not unusual for me.
50. I try very hard to be perfect.
51. Some people are perfect.
52. I have gotten so mad at people that I have worried about myself.
53. In school, I don't want to be part of any group.
54. The groups in this school are stupid.
55. I almost never feel guilty.
56. I can feel afraid, mad, and sad all at once.
57. I've felt like hurting myself on purpose.
58. Some people think I'm a nothing.
59. Some people think I'm weird.
60. I've done dangerous things, where I knew I would get hurt.
61. I believe strongly in the right to own a gun.
62. There are some secrets I will never share with anyone.
63. My secrets could get me in trouble.
64. I have secrets that would make some people think I'm crazy.
65. I've never told the truth about what somebody did to me.
66. I used to hate for certain people to give me a bath or shower.
67. There's a particular person who gives me a weird feeling.
68. Things have been done to me that I can never tell about.
69. I share a secret with a particular person.

70. Something bad happened to me that is my fault.
71. Something inside me caused another person to do something bad.
72. If I ever told the truth about what happened to me, someone would get in trouble.
73. If I ever told the truth about what happened to me, a person or a pet might be badly harmed.
74. The person I share a secret with is an adult.
75. The person I share a secret with is a child or teenager.
76. I keep thinking about my private parts.
77. I feel very hopeless about my situation.

Child Abuse Questions

36 - 45
47, 50, 56, 57, 60, 62, 63, 65,
66 – 77

Potential Aggression

1 – 35, 48 – 55, 58, 61, 63, 64, 68, 77

Examiner's Comments:

_____

_____

_____

_____

_____

_____

Substance Abuse Test for Resistant Students or Employees

When seeking to predict the possibility of violence, whether school or workplace, it can also be important to check for substance abuse. Such is the case where an employee or student has resisted positive change. This test is designed for those who have been uncooperative when other means of intervention have already been tried.

Interviewer: Insist on eye contact with each response. Mark "T" (true) or "U" (untrue) beside each question according to your personal impression.

1. Are you ever afraid that someone might think you are under the influence of drugs?
2. Do your social activities involve any type of drug use?
3. Do you ever get away from other people in order to take a drug?
4. Do you stay away from social events when drugs won't be included?
5. Do you ever take more of a prescription medicine than what is ordered?
6. Do you ever use illegal drugs on top of prescription medicines?
7. What prescription drugs do you take?
8. What is the strength of your prescription medicine, and how often do you take it?
9. Has anyone ever said you're acting strangely?
10. Does anyone suspect that you are on drugs?
11. Do you have a high tolerance for prescription medicines such as pain killers or tranquilizers? In other words, can you take a heavier dose than most people?
12. Do you use medicines to cope with stress?
13. Did you ever experiment with crack cocaine?
14. In the past year, have you changed friends or moved to a new location?
15. Do you ever feel guilty about using medicines or drugs?
16. Have you ever broken the law while under the influence of medicine or drugs?
17. Do you feel strongly that drugs should be legalized?
18. Do you have any medical condition that requires medication?

19. If answer to the last question is "yes", do you follow the doctor's instructions?
20. Have you ever been late for work or missed work due to medicines or drugs?
21. How many of your friends are drug users?
22. Are you worried about a close friend's drug use?
23. Have you had major problems with employment due to drugs?
24. Do you live at a fairly low standard?
25. Do you rely on family or close friends for housing, food, or money?
26. Have you ever had an accident that occurred while you were using?
27. Are any of your important relationships in danger of ending?
28. Do you resent authority?
29. Do you ever feel angry or defensive?
30. Do you get angry when someone asks about your drug use?
31. Do you often pay your bills late?
32. Do you come up short on money before the next pay day?
33. Do you have any disabilities that are difficult to cope with?
34. Is your stress in life greater than most people's?

16 | Workplace Violence

Much workplace violence is sparked by stalkers who come to the workplace of their victims and harass or punish them on the job. Offices, factories, assembly plants, and even schools are at risk of an intruder stopping at nothing to get to his victim. As domestic violence increases, so does workplace violence. A great deal of abuse also arises from a superior to an employee, or even from a colleague nominally on the same level. This can even amount to physical torture, but is more often verbal, including the use of "humor", the issuing of arbitrary orders, isolation, malicious gossip, etc. Violence is not always physical. Therefore, it is wise for an employer to screen his female candidates for child and domestic abuse, with the tests earlier included. The screening that follows is particularly for men but may also reveal vital traits in female applicants. In addition, it is recommended that employers administer the "Substance Abuse Screen for Resistant Drug Abusers" on p. 167.

Test for Potentially Dangerous Employees

This questionnaire requires an experienced interviewer willing to call upon professional consultation before taking any definitive action.

To be asked out loud by interviewer; response: "yes" or "no".

1. Sometimes it seems that my thoughts are broadcast so that others can hear them.
2. Others can read my thoughts.
3. I've heard voices that no one else could hear.
4. There are people who try to control my thoughts.
5. I'm the target of a conspiracy.
6. I've made plans about how to kill myself.
7. When I'm upset, I typically do something to hurt myself.
8. I have no interest in life.
9. Death would be a relief.
10. I'm considering suicide.
11. People are afraid of my temper.
12. Sometimes my temper explodes and I completely lose control.
13. Sometimes I'm very violent.
14. I've threatened to hurt people.

(Source of above items: *Personality Assessment Inventory*, Leslie Morey, Ph.D., Psychological Assessment Resources, Inc.)

15. I hope that I can retire early.
16. I only work because I have to.
17. People have wondered why I've had so many different jobs.
18. When I'm not employed, I sleep very late.
19. I'm really a night person, not a morning person.
20. I work better when left alone to do the job my own way.
21. I believe that drugs should be legalized.
22. I see nothing wrong with having a beer at lunch.
23. I'm not the kind of person who likes to join groups.
24. There is someone in my life who thinks he (or she) owns me.
25. I never have more than one or two very close friends.
26. I've broken off close relationships and then formed an intense friendship with somebody else.

27. Sometimes my mind drifts off into space, like I'm not here anymore.
28. I jump at sudden noises.
29. I have nightmares or flashbacks about past events.
30. Sometimes I think there's something wrong with my nerves.
31. I was abused as a child.
32. Fairly often, I have to ask people to repeat what they just told me.
33. People often make me repeat or explain what I've just said.
34. I think it's stupid that drugs haven't been legalized.
35. In my job history, I haven't been fired; I just quit.
36. If there was a company picnic, I probably wouldn't come.
37. I don't like doing the same job over and over again.
38. I get a lot of aches and pains when I work a long time.
39. Companies don't give enough rest breaks.
40. The supervisors I've worked for have been conceited; they think they're better than the workers.

Questions for Multi-Word Response:

41. The real reason I left my last job is because _____
42. The ideal type of job for me would be _____
43. The main things I don't like about other people are _____
44. These are some of the things my other supervisors did wrong

_____

45. The things that are wrong with this country are_____

_____

46. The reason I haven't lasted very long at jobs before is _____

_____

47. The pay and benefits for this particular job should be _____

_____

48. When I get home, here's how I spend my time_____

_____

49. The people I admire most in this world are _____ and the reasons are _____

50. The things I believe would make me a better worker are _____

_____

51. My long-term goals in life are _____

###

Interviewer's Impressions

_____

_____

_____

_____

_____

_____

_____

_____

_____

_____

_____

Consultation Indicated ____yes ____no

17 | The Falsely Accused

Victims in the Truest Sense

Falsely accused parents, usually fathers, are a rapidly growing population. The National Center for Child Abuse and Neglect reports 3.5 million cases of *alleged* child abuse in 1998, with 1 million of these *confirmed*. But 71 percent of the accusations were unfounded and *false*. (Tong, 2002).

One can only imagine the horror that a man like "David" in Chapter 10 (page 103) goes through when a child he dearly loves betrays him. Not only does he have a losing battle with a twisted court system rubber-stamping the zealous actions of the child-protective-service agency, he can never prove his innocence to the most important people in his life. Never knowing what his friends and family really think is the worst part of all.

The process goes on endlessly. Not only does the threat of jail hang over his head, but his family is destroyed. The child inventing the lies, usually in collusion with the mother, becomes only a pawn—also a victim, a weapon against a hated husband.

A great proportion of the false allegations are created by runaway teens, especially when they are running from juvenile court rather than from the father. When finally picked up by the police, they claim they ran away because they were being sexually abused by their father. Their accounts are not only detailed but disgusting, extremely graphic, and very well rehearsed, with the help of other runaways.

In most cases, the teen has been further coached by Mother, who has her own stake in the outcome; that is, custody plus the cruelest possible punishment of the father. Often the child, the mother, or both are sociopathic liars hell-bent on getting their way.

The biggest problem is that there is rarely any evidence to disprove. So what defense does the falsely accused have?

Dean Tong, author of *Elusive Innocence: Survival Guide for the Falsely Accused*, is one of the nation's best experts on how a man can win his case.

When writing this book, he asked me to contribute an appendix of questions that a defense attorney can ask during a deposition of the accusing child. The questions listed below were used successfully in a court case in Jacksonville, Florida; that is why they are not generalized. They pertain to a real case.

These interrogatories are so thorough and strong that I truly doubt that any lying teen could stand up against them. I urge most strongly that any defendant, if innocent, insist—and I mean *demand*—that his attorney ask the child *every single question*. Most of them are listed below. The full set is included as Appendix I in Tong's book.

Defense Interrogatories for Lying Accusers

1. Name all persons who have prepared you to answer questions during this session.
2. Before you ran away, did you have any intention of "getting even" with your father if he reported your absence to the police?
3. Did you disclose your plans to make up a story about your father to any of your friends?
4. How many interviewing sessions took place that dealt with accusations against your father?
5. Who conducted these interviews?
6. Did you take any tests?
7. How long did each interview last?
8. Did you take an oath to tell the truth when you were interviewed?
9. Who witnessed this oath?
10. Was a family history obtained from your mother?
11. Have you ever been sexually active with any boy or girl?
12. At what age was your first sexual experience with a boy or girl?
13. Were you ever reluctant about accusing your father?
14. Is there any benefit to you if you stick to your accusation?
15. When you made these accusations against your father, were you angry at him for other reasons?
16. If you were angry at him, why?
17. Were you angry at your mother?
18. Why were you angry at your mother?
19. When your mother took you to stay with your father, did you feel this was punishment or rejection? (Some mothers will purposely place the child in the father's care to provide a time-frame for alleged abuse.)
20. Why did you wait until your final runaway before accusing your father? Why not the first time you ran away?
21. Why did you not tell your therapist or your school counselor that your father molested you?
22. Why did you not tell your pastor or any other family member?
23. If your father really molested you, why didn't you warn your brother(s) and sister(s)?

24. What reasons can you think of that your father would take you to a counselor and a priest, and encouraged you to stay with family members and friends when you could tell any one of them that he molested you?

25. Describe in detail your memory of your father molesting you. Include the place and room, what you were wearing, what you were doing right before, what time of day it was, what he said, what you said, where he touched you and for how long, whether there was pain, how you felt, whether there was discharge or blood, whether you cried, whether you begged him to stop, and any other details that you remember. I will repeat each of these one at a time and give you time to think before you answer.

26. Please describe your most horrible memory of being abused?

27. Do you suffer from flashbacks (explain), night sweats, or nightmares due to the abuse?

28. What do you see in your nightmares and flashbacks, and how do you feel?

29. If you told your counselor other things before you ran away, why didn't you mention the abuse?

30. Have you even made any complaints to anyone about these matters, and what did you say?

31. Do you have any friends who have made similar accusations about a parent?

32. Please name other people you have had sex with, and whether they were children, teens, or adults.

33. Do you understand that any adult who had sex with you, or sheltered you while considered a runaway, will be prosecuted as a criminal?

34. You were willing to accuse your father. Are you willing to name anybody in the last question? I'll repeat it.

35. Was anyone who sheltered you a drug dealer? Anyone into "kiddie porn"?

36. Where can we find the people in the last question?

37. Do you know that lying in an interview like this one, under oath, is a crime in itself?

38. Has anyone told you what perjury is and what the penalty is?

39. Do you think your mother will benefit if your father is punished?

40. When you were still a runaway, whom did you tell about your father? How can we reach this person or these people?

41. Can you contact the people you were with during your runaway and ask them to come in?

42. If you know, please name the classification that your accusation was placed in. I'll explain each as I name them. They are:

    - Credible disclosure—suspicion of abuse supported.

    - Credible non-disclosure—no or low index of suspicion remains.

    - Non-credible disclosure—evidence of coaching or other factors decreases or removes suspicion of abuse.

    - Unclear—high index of suspicion remains, but no disclosure or problematic disclosure exists.

43. Do you feel your mother has added credibility to your accusations against your father, and if so, how?

44. What kinds of accusations has your mother made about your father to other members of the family?

45. What have you purposely not told me?

References

Alcoholics Anonymous, over 70 Years of Growth. A.A. World Services Office, New York City (2012)

Alexander, R.C. and Durfee, D.T. *Perspective of the U.S. Advisory Board on Child Abuse and Neglect,* "The APSAC Advisor, Special Issue on Child Fatalities," 7, 4 (1994)

American Psychiatric Association. *Diagnostic Criteria from DSM-IV.* Washington, D.C. (1994)

Ames, Louis B. "Child Psychology," *in Grolier's Encyclopedia (*1993)

Baumrind, D. *Parenting Styles and Adolescent Development.* In Lerner, R.M., Peterson, A.C., and Brooks-Gunn, J. (eds.) *Encyclopedia of Adolescence.* New York: Garland (1991)

Barth, Amy. *101 Tips for Survivors of Sexual Abuse: A Pocket Book of Wisdom.* Ann Arbor, MI: Loving Healing Press (2009)

Bechler, R.F. and Hudson, L. Developmental Psychology: An Introduction (1986)

Briere, J., Evans, D., Runtz, M. & Wall, T. *Symptomatology* in *Men Who Were Molested as Children: A Comparison Study.* "American Journal of Orthopsychiatry," 58 (1988)

Botash, Ann S., M.D. "Head Trauma". ChildAbuseMD.com (2012)

Castallo, M. and Ewart, H. *A Carnation a Day.* Philadelphia: Dorrance & Company, (1977)

Cerny, J. in *Human Development Guide.* http://pulua.hcc.hawaii.edu (1996)

Desjardins, Liliane, Oelklaus, N., and Watson, I. *Rewriting Life Scripts: Transformational Recovery for Families of Addicts.* Ann Arbor, MI: Life Scripts Press (2010).

Disciplining Children in America: A Gallup Poll Report, December, 1995

Egeland, B. Stroufe, L.A., and Erickson, M.F. *Developmental Consequences of Different Patterns of Maltreatment.* "Child Abuse and Neglect", 7 (1983)

Erickson, M. and Egeland, B. Throwing a Spotlight on the Developmental Outcomes for Children: Findings of a Seventeen-Year Follow-Up Study. Internet Trauma and Abuse Domain (1996).

Finkelhor, D. *A Sourcebook on Child Sexual Abuse.* Beverly Hills: Sage Publications (1989)

Frankl, V. *Man's Search for Meaning.* Washington, D.C.: Washington Square Press (1998)

FreudNet: Internet Reference Page (1996)

Fromuth, M.E. & Burkhart, B.R. Long-Term Psychological Correlates of Childhood Sexual Abuse in Two Samples of College Men. "Child Abuse and Neglect", 13 (1989)

Grohol, A. *Child Sexual Abuse.* Mental Health Domain, Internet (1996)

Heise, L. *Ending Violence Against Women.* Associated Press (1999)

Hartman, W. and Pennington, K. *The History of Byzantine Eastern Canon Law to 1500.* Washington, D.C.: Catholic University of America Press (2012)

Herman, J. *Trauma and Recovery.* New York: Basic Books (1992)

Hopper, J. *Sexual Abuse Prevalence Studies.* hopper@cybercom.net (1996)

Hotchin, S. Abuse Against Women a Health Issue. Baltimore: Associated Press (2000)

Hotchin, S. *Study: Third of All Women Abused.* Baltimore: Associated Press (2000)

Hunter, J.A. A Comparison of the Psychosocial Adjustment of Adult Males and Females Sexually Molested as Children. "Journal of Interpersonal Violence", 6 (1991)

Huyer, D. Thoracoabdominal Trauma in Child Abuse. "Perspective of the U.S. Advisory Board on Child Abuse and Neglect," The APSAC Advisor, Special Issue on Child Fatalities, 7, 4 (1994)

Kaplan, Bernard, "Developmental Psychology," in *Grolier's Encyclopedia* (1993)

Kotler, J.A. and Brown, R.W. *Introduction to Therapeutic Counseling* (2nd Ed.) Pacific Grove: Brooks/Cole (1992)

Krill, William E, McKinnon, M., and Volkman, Marian K. *Gentling: A Practical Guide to Treating Ptsd in Abused Children.* Ann Arbor, Mich: Loving Healing Press, (2011).

Lehman, B. *A Catalogue of Mennonite and Amish Resources.* Denver: Mennonite Foundation (1996)

Levinson, D.J. *A Concept of Adult Development.* "American Psychologist," 41 (1986)

Lew, M. *Victims No Longer.* New York: Nevraumont (1992)

Lisak, D. The Psychological Impact of Sexual Abuse: Content Analysis of Interview with Male Survivors. "Journal of Traumatic Stress," 7 (1994)

McKinnon, M., and Splho, M. *Repair for Teens: A Program for Recovery from Incest & Childhood Sexual Abuse.* Ann Arbor, MI: Loving Healing Press (2012)

Myers, M.D. *Men Sexually Assaulted as Adults and Sexually Abused as Boys.* 13th Annual Canadian Sex Research Forum Conference. "Archives of Sexual Behavior," 18 (1989)

Nelson, B. Internet Domain, Psychology, Abuse Pages (1996)

Olson, P.E. The Sexual Abuse of Boys: A Study of the Long-Term Psychological Effects. In Hunter, M. (Ed.) The Sexually Abused Male: Vol. 1. *Prevalence, Impact and Treatment.* Lexington, MA: Lexington Books (1990)

Peck, M. S. *People of the Lie, The Hope for Healing Human Evil.* New York: Touchstone, Simon & Schuster (1983)

Pelton, L. Issue Paper 6. National Coalition for Child Protection Reform (2011) http://www.nccpr.org/reports/6Poverty.pdf

Piaget, J. *The Moral Development of the Child* (1932; repr. 1965)

Rothbart, M.K. Temperament and the Development of Inhibited Approach. *Child Development,* 59 (1988)

Shakeshaft, C. *Sexual Abuse of Student by School Personnel.* "Phi Delta Kappan," 514 (March, 1995)

Shulman, T.E. *Child Abuse in Schools: Under Investigation.* ENWR 101, Section 8 (Fall, 1995)

Smith, W.L. *Abusive Head Injury.* "Perspective of the U.S. Advisory Board on Child Abuse and Neglect," *The APSAC Advisor,* 7, 4 (1994)

Special Issue on Child Fatalities, The APSAC Advisor. Chicago: American Professional Society on the Abuse of Children, (1994)

Tong, D. *Elusive Innocence. Survival Guide for the Falsely Accused.* Lafayette, LA: Huntington House Publishers (2005)

U.S. Department of Health and Human Services, *Child Maltreatment 1995: Reports from the States to the National Child Abuse and Neglect Data System.* Washington, D.C.: U.S. Government Printing Office (1997)

U.S. Department of Health and Human Services, *The Third National Incidence Study of Child Abuse and Neglect.* Washington, D.C.: U.S. Government Printing Office (1996)

U.S. Department of Justice, *Wives Are the Most Frequent Victims in Family Murders.* Press Release (July 10, 1994)

Walker, A.G. *Cognitive Interviewing, 2* (July/August, 1995)

Walker, A.G. *Handbook on Questioning Children: A Linguistic Perspective.* Washington, D.C.: ABA Center on Children and the Law (1994)

Warren, Richard. *The Purpose-Driven Life: What on Earth Am I Here For?* Grand Rapids, Mich: Zondervan (2002)

World Headquarters, Alcoholics Anonymous, New York, NY, Telephone interview (March, 1999); internet article by same, February, 2012.

About the Author

Most Reverend Heyward B. Ewart, III, Ph.D., D.D., has devoted more than 28 years of his professional life to the protection and treatment of women, children, and the family. During the Carter administration, he served the White House Conference on Families, and such leadership continues to this day. He is not only a veteran clinician in the mental health field, but also a distinguished teacher at the university level and an active chaplain. His audio and video lectures have been used by distance-learning students across the United States and in some 41 foreign countries.

A Diplomate of the American College of Forensic Examiners, he has served as an expert trial witness in several states. He has also conducted continuing education at the University of North Florida and University Hospital of Jacksonville, FL.

Archbishop Ewart is President and Academic Dean of St. James the Elder Theological Seminary, an institution offering degrees in psychology and theology through distance learning combined with personal mentorship by recognized experts. The Seminary boasts the lowest tuition rates of any comparable institution. Their curricula span from the bachelor's level to the doctorate. [http://stjamestheelderseminary.org] He welcomes and tries to answer emails via father22@live.com.

A much sought-after public speaker, Dr. Ewart is a commanding presenter who speaks with great passion on the issues of abused women and children. He has hosted and appeared as a guest on many TV and radio programs in major markets, a love that dates back to his original career as a radio and TV news announcer.

He is a published poet, author of three books, besides this one, and his hobbies also include photography, singing, drama, and social activities of all kinds.

Index

A

B

C

D

V

Coping with Physical Loss and Disability:
A Workbook by Rick Ritter, MSW

Do You Have A Loved One with Disabilities?

This workbook provides more than 50 questions and exercises designed to empower those with physical loss and disability to better understand and accept their ongoing processes of loss and recovery. The exercises in *Coping with Physical Loss and Disability* were distilled from ten years of clinical social work experience with clients suffering from quadriplegia, paraplegia, amputation(s), cancer, severe burns, AIDS, hepatitis, lupus, and neuro-muscular disorders arising from. Whether the physical loss arises from accidents, injury, surgery, or disease, the techniques in this new workbook are guaranteed to improve functioning and well-being.

Praise *for Coping with Physical Loss and Disability*

"This workbook is a very good stimulus for focusing on issues that are crucial for better coping with loss and disability."
—Beni R. Jakob, Ph.D, Israeli Arthritis Foundation (INBAR)

"This workbook is a tremendous resource that is practical and easy to use. The author shows his connection with this material in a way from which we can all benefit. —Geneva Reynaga-Abiko, Psy.D., Clinical Psychologist, Urbana-Champaign Counseling Center

"To date I have not seen another tool that can help people who have disabilities become self-aware and adjust to their new lives as well as this workbook does. This workbook can help them to see how they still have strengths and abilities and move beyond being disabled to reestablish their self-acceptance and functionality." —Ian Landry, MSW, RSW

"Rick Ritter is able to provide us with an insightful road map to the growth process of individuals experiencing physical loss. As clinicians we often need to provide support to those who have experienced much more loss than we ever can imagine. This workbook is a masterpiece in helping us accomplish that proficiency." —Darlene DiGorio-Hevner, LCSW

Loving Healing Press 5145 Pontiac Trail
Ann Arbor, MI 48105
(734)662-6864
info@LovingHealing.com

124 pp — $17.95 Retail
ISBN-13 978-1-932690-18-7
Includes biblio., resources, and index.

http:/www.PhysicalLoss.com

Life Skills:
Improve the Quality of Your Life with Metapsychology.

Life Skills, by Marian K. Volkman, is the first ever self-help book based on Metapsychology techniques. Based on the work of Frank A. Gerbode, M.D., *Life Skills* makes use of one-on-one session work to achieve the individual's personal goals -- from relieving past pain to living more fully to expanding consciousness.

- Learn handy and usually quite fast techniques to assist another person after a shock, injury or other distress.
- Learn simple methods for expanding your awareness on a daily basis.
- Gain a deeper understanding of what a relationship is, and how to strengthen and nurture it.
- Learn the components of successful communication, what causes communication to break down, and how to repair breakdowns.
- Learn an effective tool for making important life decisions.

Praise *for Life Skills*

"*Life Skills* is replete with examples, exercises, episodes from the author's life, and tips—this is a must for facilitators, clients, and anyone who seeks heightened emotional welfare—or merely to recover from a trauma.
    —Sam Vaknin, PhD, author of *Malignant Self Love*

"*Life Skills* is a serious, impressive, and thoughtful work with one objective in mind: teaching how to reach one's full potential in practical, pragmatic, easy-to-follow steps that will literally change one's life."
    —James W. Clifton, M.S., Ph.D.,

"*Life Skills* by Marian Volkman is not to be read once and then put away. It is a guide to living a full, satisfactory life, a philosophy, a challenge. If you take the trouble to do the exercises the way the author suggests, they will change your life."   —Robert Rich, Ph.D., M.A.P.S.,

Loving Healing Press
5145 Pontiac Trail
Ann Arbor, MI 48105
(734)662-6864
info@LovingHealing.com

180 pp — $16.95 Retail
ISBN-13 978-1-932690-05-7
Includes biblio., resources, and index.

http:/www.LifeSkillsBook.com

www.ingramcontent.com/pod-product-compliance
Lightning Source LLC
Chambersburg PA
CBHW072221270326
41930CB00010B/1938